To myself

Contents

The Creation of Experience 1

The First Self 3

The Next Self 13

    Consciousness 18

The Mind 21

Dreams 27

    Angels 33

Spirit 37

    The Etheric Body 41

    Schumann Frequencies 43

The Formation of the Creator 45

Universe 47

    Time 48

    Light 50

    Energy 51

    Dimensions 52

One Turning

One Turning

Universus

Edmund Wood

Copyright © 2020 Edmund Wood
All rights reserved.
ISBN: 979-8-5634-2316-9

God 53

Life 63

The Edge of the Universe 67

   The Present 68

   Interest 71

The Realizing of the Form 73

Purpose 75

   Earth Consciousness 78

Heaven 85

Society and the Divine 89

Language 97

The Experience of Reality 101

Reality 103

Love 109

The White Room 113

Soul 119

The Meaning of Life 127

The Creation of Experience

Our minds describe and analogize what we receive through sensation.
Our experience is this conceptualization.
Our description only a simile;
something compared to something else.

Comparing one thing with another,
defining ad infinitum;
separating what is one
- the universe -
into an infinite language of definition.

All experience is the minds conceptualizing of sensation.
The concept is described and defined and deformed by language.
Reality per se cannot be described;
there is only the comparing of experiences;
a cornucopia of relativity.

All the separation at the end of the day is just words.
All we do is create a story.

Uni-verse: One Story

One Turning

The Creation of Experience

The First Self

To get to the core of understanding what this existence is, is to get to the core of ourselves and recognise that there has never been anyone better to see this than ourselves, because everyone else is our self at our core.

I know who you were at the beginning, because there is no individual there then—that comes later—and you being there was me being there too. I know who you are now too, at your very core, because I am there too, just as you are here within me. But your 'self' is the individual that exists in the physical, together with its mental peculiarities developed from its existence. This is who you are too, and I do not know that you, and can only guess at who you are in that being by using any similar experiences from my own life. The whole of you, physical and original, is unique. The core of you is the same in everyone.

The accessing of this core knowledge lies in our very early lives and our memories from this era is our pure source to find our true story. I have a hundred memories of being a baby, but my earliest memory is perhaps the most important to me, because it is a window to who I am without any clutter getting in the way. It exposes consciousness, bared and separate to the mind which grows from it.

My first extended memory was becoming aware of something building up and getting stronger, within an otherwise black void. As it intensified, I recognized that it had happened before (possibly more than once) and knew that as it continued I had previously lost awareness of it. I was determined that this time I would follow it completely to see what happens next. It was a deliberate effort to follow this sensation and remain aware of it as it grew stronger, and I persevered until there was the result of being ejected into being a baby crying.

There were people in the room, though they seemed to me like aliens, and it was very bright, and I thought "oh, this again!", though without the words, obviously. I sort of knew it, even though it was very strange. I observed the whole of this process dispassionately, with a recognition and a sort of "aha!" feeling, as my perseverance paid off. It was certainly familiar; I had been here before.

I believe it was the act of crying that had led to the cessation of awareness on the previous occasion, like losing consciousness during extreme pain, which was why it took such great effort to follow the sensation. There was no experience of discomfort, however. My consciousness was entirely separate from the experience, and the crying was entirely an automatic biological response to whatever the cause was; there was no suffering there as we know it. It was as if the baby that was crying was not me, more of a portal. My awareness was distinct from the physical being; I did not know that I was a baby. I did not identify the human being as being me, though later I would do, and now have difficulty not doing so. The baby is not a human being, it is just a being, a point of consciousness. The rest of its life is about being human.

What is amazing is that even at this time of life we are curious, and my determination to follow the sensation was probably my first thought, a recognition of something triggering an action of purposefulness. The base of ourselves is inquisitiveness. This must have been my first desire. I must also have been aware at this time of the transience of awareness. This experience is the arising of the mind, the experience of time. The realizing that change was occurring (past), and something else was about to happen (future).

It is the mind which compares and consequently produces the concept of time and the continuity, and with it the dichotomy that produces the self. The base beneath the mind is endless, blissful void, that is necessarily timeless. This is 'with the knowing'—consciousness (con = with, scio = knowing).

Base consciousness is the state without sensory information. The mind arises with the processing of the senses. The mind creates an experience which is a construction of continuity, and I access this as memory and this memory is me.

~

I am sure that many others have had this memory and equate it with being born, except I know that it wasn't the first time because of my preceding thought to follow it. Which for others again, may strengthen their belief in reincarnation precisely because it isn't the first time, or it may be that these experiences gave rise to their concept of reincarnation in the first place! It must be realized that no one has a clear empirical understanding of reincarnation, death etc.—it is all indoctrinated supposition, garnered and collated from fleeting glimpses of unverifiable experience.

The backdrop landscape that this occurs in, the blackness of base consciousness, seems infinite. It seems like aeons pass. There is so much time because there is no time, and no worry, no care at all. This is limbo or purgatory, and not at all unpleasant. Whether this is just the beginnings of life and the experience of existence without the comparing of things which the mind does, and so seem infinite due to a lack of boundary, or it is a period between lives in the reincarnation story, is possibly unknowable. I prefer the former however, as all the stories of reincarnation involve an adult mind in the story telling, with the inevitable societal indoctrination permeating the experience.

This prior first experience with infinite existence and no care, is the base consciousness that is the divine and the place to just be. Return to this first state for salvation; this is the sacred state which cannot be desecrated and where we go when we meditate and are in deep sleep. It is always there waiting for us. It is there right now, happening beneath all our happenings. Everything else in our lives has all been about acquiring skills to better be. It is the watcher that is completely independent of it all that is the original you, and possibly the most important thing.

Consciousness means *'with* knowing' because it is the mind that knows, and this consciousness is just *with* it. It doesn't play any part, it's like it's just along for the ride. The base of it. Your consciousness is always pure, and inquisitiveness arises from it—the mind. It is not separate from the mind, but the basest part of it, the intensive root. With no past or future and therefore no physical link, it is indistinguishable from any others consciousness and consequently has no individuality.

The meaning of consciousness is this *'with'* the 'knowing'. It is the 'with', that is the defining part of consciousness. It is this that forms the core or base of the later building of the ego and self-awareness and the concept maker. The separation of the 'with' and the 'knowing' is key to this.

Consciousness experiences sensation as an indistinct spiritual thing. It is the mind that intellectualises (inter-lego—between the gathering) and modularises experiences, later forming them into words. Behind the words, below the mind, before mental awareness (pre-sentia, the present), is the spiritual experience called consciousness.

~

It could be that the very first awareness of something is not rememberable. Perhaps it is only the second time that it happens that there is the actual means of remembering it. This only occurs very early on in our lives, as all new experiences are now just a variation of already experienced phenomena, and there are enough neural connections to do the job. But the very first time, is the first laying down of a neural pathway, and it takes a repeating of it for it to become the memory. This memory occurs because there was a previous occasion and is only existent because of it, and is in fact, *it*, because memory is ultimately just a replaying of a neural pattern.

This first memory of mine being aware of sensation, and the anticipation and concept forming, is the First Self. The 'waiting' that is before it, seems eternal and is the base state, but it is not 'self'. This is identical to all sentient life (some say to everything, though without qualification). Base consciousness is identical in every human being. Here there is absolutely no individual. When there is an individual, that is in the physical, and then there can be a comparing, and there is a self and another. Therefore, the self is not base consciousness. The self is the physical body, and the mind that has arisen from it. The word self is personal by definition, not something which is common to everybody. That word would be soul.

It is the sensation that unlocks the individuality and produces a mind of comparisons. The mind forms from the neural pathways that are laid down from the sensation that comes from exposure to living. It is this mind that is the self, and each one is unique. The awareness of sensation and the curiosity to follow it, is the First Self. The First Self does not have control of the body at this point. It can only follow and cannot lead; it just observes. My memory of it is that it doesn't even care if it takes part or not. The choice of following the sensation, the baby that was crying, and the world outside of it, were nothing more than a side-track. An idle curiosity. It didn't have to participate, and actually couldn't anyway.

∼

Science (the stem 'scie' is the same as 'scio' in con<u>scio</u>usness, meaning knowing), says that as the hippocampus (a part of the brain which is involved in memory), is not developed in the baby, that it is not possible to remember anything from this era of our lives. I know that is not correct, and I believe it is because the hippocampus is used for the ego, and the ego has no purpose for existing until society interaction kicks in. Everything grows according to its usage. This is probably why so few others can remember being a baby, because they are locked within the matrix of a society and the ego that is created for it. My extreme level of isolation has allowed me to bypass this aspect to a certain extent.

It is further complicated by the fact that imagination uses the same neural pathways as memory, and you can therefore create false memories. There is a difficulty in investigating it without contaminating it, which makes it necessary for very careful treading in memory retrieval. But perhaps my discovery of this room with people in it, which I emerged into as a crying baby, was a bit of a disappointment to me. My thought might have been "oh, not this again! I don't want to do this again". But this would be my attitude now, like it is for all the guru's that wish to transcend the reincarnation cycles, and might be a retrospective addition to the experience. Once we have had this interpretation it is impossible to know whether we are making it up or not. To separate memory from imagination might not be possible.

From other experiences I have had of this First Self though, I am sure there would actually have been no judgement whatsoever, and I wouldn't even have cared. Life is not something to cling to at this stage or reject. It really just doesn't matter; it is so unimportant.

I think the reason why I can remember being a baby, is that I can remember meditating when I was a baby, by becoming aware that I was getting carried away by experience and deliberately refraining from it. This centring of awareness is a detachment from getting lost in it, and possibly preserves some of the neurological pathways for memory of that era.

∼

We expect the core consciousness—the enlightened state of awareness, to be holy and penetrating, but it is possible to visualize it being a disinterested slob, who has no opinion whatsoever, and just sits there vacantly, hardly paying any attention at all. Or is that just me!

It is the mind that brings the intensity of interest to the party. The core cannot appreciate anything. It has no judgement; it is the mind that does all that. The word interest (inter = between, est = to be: between being), refers to the activity of the mind bouncing about upon the backdrop of base consciousness, and it is that that we try to control during meditation. We will try to fill every moment of our day with this interest, but we are always inevitably forced into sleep, and a return to base consciousness, to just being. This state of dreamless deep sleep is rarely remembered because it is only the 'interest' that the mind does, that is the actual 'remembering'. There are no 'members' to make again (re), in the state of base consciousness.

But I can be aware during deep sleep, and as a child was always aware through these unconscious periods. I was always confused by what the adults were talking about when they said "unconscious", as it is the same as conscious. It is just without the ability to do anything, think anything, or care about anything. There is just nothing to remember of it except its amazing nothing.

That which is truly sacred is incapable of being desecrated. This is the true centre; the absolute present where no stories are being told.

The 'self' is a personal pronoun that refers to the physical being and the awareness that is generated from that, and is an autonomous entity of being which is individual, and not the core awareness which exists throughout all sentient beings, which is called consciousness. It is important to understand and maintain the boundaries of these words.

Base consciousness is the base neural mechanism at work without any sensory input or activity, or using previous sensory input in the network. It is the idling of an engine not in gear. It is important to note that this consciousness is the core of experience and not the core of the universe. All that can be experienced is consciousness, but this does not mean that everything *is* consciousness. The concepts that are perpetuated by this misunderstanding are caused by guru's repeating their guru's words. I have not had a guru; I have trusted that the universe will reveal all to me. I am my own Hogwarts!

~

Everyone has to come to terms with the discovery that you are not the only divine being in the universe. It's a memory that can be buried deep, but somewhere in your early life the realization was there, and had to be deferred to such a degree, that all knowledge of it is lost in the societal shroud. And so, if rediscovered, it will be realized that we all have access to this divine memory, before we were restricted to just our social selves. Some have kept this knowing, but always have to keep quiet about it.

You really need to get back to your first experience of it to fully understand it. It is only through actual experience can there be knowing in this case. To know who we are, it is really helpful to remember our first experiences because they are untainted by later influences.

You have to start with a true seed. If your seed comes from someone else, it is tainted by their society and that person's habits and beliefs, and even by the attempted communication of it. It is just not good enough. The true seed is within yourself. There is no one else who has a truer seed. No one else can tell you who you are. The purity of it is in the first 2 or 3 years of your life, after that it is contaminated with the false understandings of others. You cannot trust them. None of them have anything else more than you at your core self, and unpolluted self. Anyone saying something holy which comes from another, is not being holy; they are pretending.

What I know is extracted from the very source. There is no clear truth in the eclectic assemblage of other's concepts; what a nightmare of disambiguating and unravelling that would be. Impossible! It is a ridiculous thing to do to tell someone else's story. There is only one story—yourself. There is nothing out there except the mechanism that is creating it. That is why it doesn't matter if you die, because the same life is effectively happening to all the same beings out there, just in a different location and time. This is what is meant by consciousness being eternal—it carries on in other individual units like yourself, as it already is doing. Time is not strictly linear in this context, and future and past get jumbled together by the brain into a story which doesn't always quite fit.

If you cannot remember the first 2 years of your life, the 2 foremost important years upon which the whole of your life is built upon; the foundation of all your emotions and the root definition of who you are; if you cannot remember this, how can you know who you truly are? You have amnesia!

My First Self would have been your experience too. There is no individual developed at this point. That is created by the sequence of events that happens to the physical individual afterwards, and the responses that that core individual makes in interaction to those events. Your unique DNA will influence this building of you and create the individual character and person that you have become, but it will not affect the core consciousness.

The 'First Self' consciousness experience that I can remember must be identical for everyone. That is why it is significant, and I can't believe it is not at the core of every religion or philosophy, because it is pure and divine. It is the start point for everything that happens to you afterwards. It is unpolluted, it is the true you, who you really are. It is devoid of any social indoctrination, which cannot be said for any later experiences.

~

The Next Self
~ Ego ~

'Who' you are, by definition, can only be relative to others. It is the distinction that exists between you and everyone else, that defines 'you'. The areas in which those distinctions exist, define the boundaries of the definition of you.

The self-comparative mechanism which the brain produces to achieve this identification is called the ego—the Latin and Greek word for 'self'. The ego could also be defined as the conceptualised self, as opposed to the purely existent self. The conceptualised self comprises of what has happened in the past and what you might be in the future all wrapped up into a fictional present. The existent self is who you actually are at that present moment, without any judgement being made to quantify or qualify that self—the true self or First Self. The true self by this definition, is beyond description, as any attempt to do so is fraught with judgement and belief systems, which end up making it subjective and ultimately untrue.

So, if for the purpose of definition, we divide ourselves into our true selves and our false selves, then the false self will be the part which has become habitualised into following patterns influenced by an unknowing society, and the true self will be the divine entity that is just existing and observing. The true self is the natural self, the part unsoiled by silly games.

If you are cognisant of yourself, that self is ego (false self). When you are your true self, that god cannot even see the fool ego. Higher awareness is just awareness without the ego. The ego dulls us like a dark filter laid over the pure brilliance of our true selves. It is this true self that we truly want to be, because that is when we are just being the universe, and the universe doesn't have any problems. All problems come from ego and society and the expectations inculcated by it. Ego is a social conformity mechanism and is rooted in caring about the opinions of others. This caring is insecurity by definition, even if you are puffing yourself up by putting others down.

You can't have an accurate concept of yourself; it always involves the perspective from another, even if that another is you. Ego always involves another's perspective, a seeing of oneself from the perception of oneself or another. It is never real.

You could look at it so that the First Self is the same as the ego but without the affectations that have been picked up along the way, because the detached observer is also the lost in it reveller, just without these patterns attached. It is these patterns that are the ego. Having no affectations is the encapsulation of the pure self; the affectations are mostly from the society and are created by the mind.

~

If the ego is the false self, then the true self without its help would have long ago stumbled over a cliff and died on the jagged rocks below, as you are your true self when a baby, which is totally trusting and free from care, but vulnerable in the world. The care of the mother and father can of course prevent the cliff fall, but as the baby grows up it needs an internal parental care for the occasions when they are not there. This self-caring mechanism is the ego; this is its purpose. The mothering aspect of it will boost self-opinion, keeping it safe from the derogatory opinions of others, while the fathering aspect will not allow social suicide and keep behaviour in line with what is acceptable in society, (or the other way around).

The ego is a protective mechanism, and by so being it is also inevitably a restricting mechanism. Just like real parents and our social indoctrination, it needs to be transcended.

The conceptualising of this 'self', is a judgement subject to comparative observations involving others, and necessarily focuses upon certain aspects and overlooks others. The aspects that are focused upon are often those that the society has deemed desirable and are therefore relative to the development and maintenance of that society. The concept that is formed, because of the generalisation, is apt to be false and hence the term false self. Conversely the true self is where no self-judgement is being made, and the natural processes are free to be expressed without the hindrance that self-observation brings.

My ego is always trying to be what I was in the past, or what I can be in the future. To be what I am in the present requires no defence. To be what I am now is the unassailable truth. The justification of myself now is simply a story of the past and my hopes for the future. All conceptualization is the mind using past and future; truly being in the present allows freedom from the ego.

The ego of a person is often meant to refer to the over evaluation of themselves, while the under evaluation may be called timidity, but both are forms of insecurity and both of these are the wrong concept of ourselves. Our self-doubt will inhibit us and prevent us from utilizing our true selves, slowing down our progress. Over evaluation tries to quicken things up, eventually producing frustration and dissatisfaction; and hence the correct concept is always now, here in the present without any concepts, because they are either going to be too little or too much; slowing it down or speeding it up, neither of which are true. Therefore, the correct concept of oneself is no concept. The true ego is no ego. The true self is no self. No story will set you free.

~

One of my first memories of ego was walking down the corridor of my infants school, at the age of 4 or 5, to go to my mum's class where she was teaching some older children. I remember getting to the door and not being able to reach the handle, and so when I knocked and was told to come in, all I could do was stand there and wait. I then used to sit on mum's lap while she read a story to the other children, who all thought I was adorable.

The awareness that the children were looking at me, made me self-conscious which made me want to avoid this ego producing situation which made me try and hide from it, eliciting "ahs" from the children and the appellation of being shy. But I wasn't trying to hide from the children's attention on me, I was trying to escape the ego arising within me. It made me squirm with uncomfortableness; I disliked it intensely and wanted to run away.

On my way to the classroom, I had met a teacher coming the other way, who stopped me to ask where I was going, as classes had already started. Before I was stopped, I was aware that I was doing something that was not normal and became self-conscious when I saw the teacher. I remember that I had had this experience of self-consciousness before and that I didn't like it. I remember actively trying to dismiss the experience and knew that it wasn't

The Creation of Experience

good. I *think* I can remember knowing a previous life where this was the norm and that I vowed I would not be like that this time, but this might be retrospective overlaying, or it could be a mix of memory and future projection formed in this life, or even knowledge of the future seeping in. But I was aware of how overwhelmingly caught up in it you can become and how unreal it was. I was aware of how affecting of your life it was. I was aware of how it should be avoided at all cost. I was even frightened of it.

I have noticed this in my cat too. When I played with her, she would invariably become self-conscious at some point, and then distract herself from it by stopping playing and vigorously cleaning herself instead. It is a good tactic and I copy it by distracting myself by focusing strongly into sensation, usually my breathing. Licking myself really doesn't do it for me!

But this self-consciousness was a bit like cheating the true reality, and felt wrong, as if I was fouling my divine self. As the teacher was talking to me, I was thinking how does he manage to control this state of self-awareness, and can he see mine? But of course, he wasn't controlling it at all, and had spent almost his entire life in that state, to the point that he didn't even realise it, and this is the norm for nearly everyone. It is the social conformity mechanism at work, the thing I have been trying to avoid all my life.

~

The actual self is relative to its environment. You behave differently according to your circumstances. Your mother, a baby and a mate are all interacted with differently, with you assuming a mode of interaction different to each. Your modal response can be humble and contrite in one situation, and arrogant and obnoxious in another. All these 'selves' are mechanisms to allow you passage through a particular social event, with the ego reacting to the environment it is in and producing a state of operation which is moderated by the particular aspects suited to it, or previously performed in it, and so is effectively a modular of characteristics. These characteristics may persist beyond the event to become an acquired personality, a habitual affectation gained from adapting oneself to its environment. It also happens with ageing, with the adoption of certain types of behaviour and mannerisms which you didn't have before; the ego of old age.

Each environment will produce an ego capable of maintaining its survival, acquiring attributes that favour that circumstance and creating a character to which you can be bound to in that circumstance. Ultimately, we have to pay homage to society, but in every environment a different ego emerges according to the different needs to survive in the new rules. The organism will find its easiest path to accomplish what it sees as its goal, which is always a form of survival.

The ego could be seen as a pattern of previous habits which the mind forms into a definition of oneself. Aspects of your life that can be encapsulated. They usually include future extrapolations too. Your very core self—the First Self, isn't yourself at all; it is everyone. What becomes identifiable as me or you, we can then later deny as even being the real us.

Consciousness

This word 'self' is reflexive and refers to person, but it is not consciousness. The consciousness that lies at the base of each person has no judgement or concept forming; it is the witness or observer, and before any mental processing, and it is only upon the activity of the mind does identity of self occur.

The Creation of Experience

Consciousness is created just by the brain being there; it is the result of the brain existing. The idling engine before it is put into gear by the mind. It is the activity of the base neuronal exchanges that produces it. Recursion without data.

The extrapolation of consciousness to non-sentient objects is a fantasy of the mind, a construction by the mind, and not verifiable experience. It comes from the observation of limitlessness due to lack of boundary in the experience, and then retrospectively applying this to the universe as it is also a boundary less base, and then extending this concept to everything within it. Core consciousness is at the base of experience, and it is an assumption of the mind that makes it the base of the universe too. It does feel like this when everything is experienced as one, and I understand why the paradigm exists, but this concept may be better applied to a base functioning of the planet rather than of the universe itself, which I expound upon later.

There certainly cannot be any experience or awareness without the accompaniment of this substrate of core consciousness, but to equate it with the underlying universe and call it eternal is entirely without qualification even though it may seem like it. This might be conceived of as the mind of God, but it is our own mind that we are experiencing as it produces a fiction of our experience. There is an impossibility to verify the origin of consciousness empirically due to the fact that as soon as any concept is produced, that will be the mind doing it. As soon as you zoom in to take a closer look, there is something else there then. This is why it cannot be described—there is an uncertainty principle at work.

The core substrate of the universe is energy, not consciousness. The quantum fixing of reality by observation cannot be the method that has created the universe up to this point of there being observers in it to do that observing, and that process of creation is still happening. Consciousness is the root of the creation of experience, not physical reality. Consciousness is the root of the story telling, not the 'One Story'.

After you die, reincarnation states that you carry on in the form of another being. But that being is any of the beings that are actually alive now, because this part that carries on, is already there. The only way you can really die, is if every being dies. You carry on through the lives of others because the base of you is the same in everyone—consciousness. The individual base you, that you consider to be the true foundation of you—the First Self, is also in everyone else—right now. The individual and its character traits that accompany this are engendered by the process of living, and are part of the physical being that dies, and die with it. The consciousness that survives, survives because it is already existing in others—it doesn't travel like an entity; that is pure fiction. This core consciousness is what we also call the soul, and everyone has the same one. Here we have the overlapping of the term's soul, consciousness and self.

The creation of experience is the product of the bodies sensory mechanisms morphed into concepts by the brain. The creator is the mind, and the formation of this creator is a story that separates what the mind makes up from what has made up the mind.

~

The Mind

It is difficult to get anything more than a spiritual amorphous concept of the neurological matrix of the brain. The creation of our minds would almost certainly begin before birth, in a gradual process as the increase in production of new neurons stimulate any existing neural pathways already made, and create a simultaneous linking up of these neurons in a symbiotic and dual causal way. As sensory information increases, the brain develops and orders itself by means of creating an interconnected matrix resulting from this stimulation, which constructs an associated neurological phenomenon from the patterns it develops, which is a recursive awareness. The being of the processes, its very existence and sum of the whole thing, is consciousness.

When senses have formed sufficiently to become a normal processing of information, the mechanism—which is patterned neuron interconnectivity—attains the capability to produce thoughts or ideas. These thoughts are packets of neural activity—modules, juxtaposed and assembled from the comparing of previous patterns of sensory information. Any experience we have is ultimately derived from sensory input and therefore any mental conceptualisation will use a synaesthesia of these senses, borrowing from the neural patterns already laid down due to exposure to living. The activity of the comparing that naturally occurs from all of this, is called the mind. It is the mechanism of knowing.

One Turning

The mind is the sensory collector which combines all that is received and merges it together to form concepts. The mind itself is created from our neurological processes which produce our experiences. The mind is effectively physically constructed from the sensory experience by the forming of neural pathways. Without something happening the mind would have no relativity to construct anything; but just being alive is something happening, and all that work being done to exist, is the energy that the brain transforms into root mind—consciousness.

Other than pure neural phenomena, everything that anyone experiences is a conceptualisation formed in the brain ultimately taken from sensory information. Our experience is therefore the past. Experience is the minds encapsulation of sensory reception. All experience is created by the brain and the usage of this experience is the mind. All other knowledge comes from the experience of others, who are as us—fallible, societally indoctrinated, confined to judgement relative to their experience, and hopelessly anthropocentric.

The mind conceptualises our reality using sensory information placed upon a framework of time, revealing a sequence of events. The mind works with patterns: in recognising relationships between things and the comparing that follows, and the noticing of the changes that this produces. It is the creator of the concepts of future, past and present, and all thoughts that reside within this compass. The patterns that are created within this neurological matrix are strengthened relative to the frequency of use, creating habits and beliefs.

~

The Creation of Experience

There is no future, there is no past; only the present, at which the mind is conceptualising future and past to act as stabilizers to gain a clearer view. Past and future are concepts only. Reality itself is only a concept of the mind.

It is our mind and the game that it produces for our awareness that is our experience of life. At the base level where we are truly flowing beneath our mind's conceptualisation, nothing much is happening. It is only the forward thinking, past and future concepts formed by the mind which makes it interesting (between our being) and in reaction, neurotransmitters and other system responses are produced which give us our physical experience. It is all just happening, and it is our reaction that produces our experience and feeds the story that we say it is.

The sensory information which enters the brain—the actual happening of this process via neurons—is what produces the artefact of experience, which when grouped with other processes, constitutes the difference that produces the functioning of the mind. It is the mind which compares and consequently produces the concept of time and the continuity.

Our sensory information is what our minds have been constructed from, but there is a substratum that is invisible to normal experience which tells the rest of the story. This substratum is the spiritual; early partially formed mental concepts, still formed from sensory input, but which are usually not relayed to our normal awareness due to their incomplete nature. The normal awareness of ours is heavily societally influenced, and if there is no association to link with, an experience can become invisible to it. This is why it is difficult to fit a spiritual experience into our normal conceptual matrix: it is too amorphous. Our awareness is an edited sub-section of experience, and the spiritual is part of what has been edited out. The mind has considerably more to access than what our awareness shows us.

One Turning

~

The mind is the result of information which then produces more. It creates the concepts and there is no experience which isn't concept. The mind focuses upon difference. That is its entire preserve. No difference, no mind. The mind exists because of the results of the difference.

New is always an attraction to this machine and it is 'interest' that is the natural motivating incentive and what the mind is attuned to. Mental stimulation occurs when there are more interconnections within the neuronal structure due to new information arriving, which then sparks off a chain reaction of neural activity, feeding recursively from previously laid down pathways which are the strengthened neural connections born from experience.

If the neurological pathways for memory and imagination are the same, then perhaps memory and imagination actually are the same. It is known that the sub-conscious does a phenomenal amount of work to do something as simple as raise a cup to one's mouth, and so it is possible that to retrieve a memory, the mind does a sort of reverse engineering and imagines what happened. I can remember this from my childhood when I was asked to remember something but all I could do was to imagine it and was then told that that was right. This 'imagining' is effectively a replaying of neural activity, and the memory is a repeat stimulation of the actual neural pathway that has previously been taken.

There is no specific location for the store of memories with this view, only an extrapolation of the path that would have to have been taken previously to get here. The same method is used to view the future, and the minds recognition of these imaginations is not always divided accurately into past and future. The mind is conceptualising all of this all the time. Time is a concept for the mind to use to understand the present. It imagines the future and the past, and the processes with which it does this do not necessarily differentiate the two as clearly as we would like to believe.

∼

When I was a toddler, my eldest sister used to take on the role of teaching me how the world worked. One day she was teaching me the difference between things moving and not moving, by rolling a ball to demonstrate movement and another object (which I can't remember exactly) to demonstrate not moving. But the object which was not moving was to my eyes moving in a wavy manner, and was definitely not, not moving. This was the common way I saw things then, and still can. The stillness that she was trying to demonstrate, did not exist to me. Even the floor and walls were moving! I remember her getting a bit annoyed with me, but I was being completely honest—the stationary object was moving, but I didn't have the language to be able to describe it or explain it.

The phenomenon is due to a state of awareness that I still possess, in which I am able to, at will, turn off the automatic correction of eye abnormalities that the mind makes, and see things as the eye itself really sees them. To see things without the minds filtering. This is best described as wavy and distorting—everything in constant motion, bending and flowing back and forth. Presumably this is due to the gelatinous nature of the eyeball which is constantly being deformed slightly within the eye socket. It can also be rhythmically jerky, which is due to the eye being vibrated by the heartbeat. These are all very unhelpful whilst in locomotion, and are quickly denigrated by the mind as we grow up, into a stable and helpful rendition of our surroundings. I believe the morphing effect may be the same as experienced by people on LSD, though I have never taken any. To walk while seeing like this is like being at sea and is most perturbing—as if it wasn't difficult enough when you are just learning how to walk anyway! I think that toddlers are unsteady on their feet due to the rolling nature of their vision as much as it is due to their unfamiliarity of physical balancing.

Seeing everything as it really is, is a revealing of one of the veils of illusion, albeit a very useful illusion. The filtering that the mind makes creates our reality. This is the creation of experience and its very nature is illusion.

The same stripping of consciousness can be done with hearing, where all sound loses its objective nature and is experienced as a sort of graduated hiss, though I find this a lot more difficult to do. It is also very difficult to see words as the abstract shapes they really are, and how we used to be able to see them before we were taught to read. These are just some of the things that our minds have distorted reality for the purpose of usefulness. How many are we unaware of?

The almost impossibility to see it as it really is—without the filtering that the mind does, shows us the extent of the illusion that we are engrossed in. This pervades throughout our lives like a dream.

∼

The Creation of Experience

Dreams

I've always liked being lost in it—abandoned to nature and its true way—who doesn't? The point of this losing it, is to exit the social conformity and enter into a different state of mind where we are free from the normal constrictions. Sleep is the only time that we are completely abandoned to it; all waking time has survival deep in its root as its ulterior motive, subtly influencing things unbeknownst to us. The society is now the survival mechanism, and so nearly all our actions are guided by it at some level, when awake.

The sleeping dream is so much more the true base, uninfluenced by space and gravity. The place where we started from, pre-birth. The separations evolving from comparisons, all come post-birth.

When we dream, our sensory inputs are switched off, but when they are switched back on when we awake, we assume that the dream mechanism also stops. I believe that when we awake from a dream, the dream does not stop; it is just that our awareness has been overwhelmed with sensory information which drowns out the dream, but it is still continuing to a degree, subtly underneath. The dream space is one without sensory load. Inhibitory mechanisms shut down most of the normal waking state and create a nice quiet environment for the mind to play in. This blank page allows us to become aware of the sub processes of the mind, and it is these processes which manifest into dreams, and are I believe happening all the time (to a degree and within a cyclical pattern), and are influencing our waking hours at a low level. I think thoughts are part of this mechanism, which implies that some kinds of thoughts are actually dreams. We are not quite as awake as we like to think we are.

It isn't one mysterious process ending and a different one beginning when we wake up, it is the same thing happening all the way through. The difference is the sensory information we get when we are awake, and this allows the continuity while awake to differentiate the two states. The consciousness and awareness of self that underlies it all, continues and remains unbroken throughout both experiences, as can be verified by lucid dreaming and the results of meditation.

The dreaming mechanism is derived from the normal brain processing of the senses, and so effectively it is all a dream—a construct of imagination. The dreams continue in the background while we are awake and alter our course in the dream we call waking. There is continuity in the waking dream, which there isn't in the sleeping. To make that continuity is a construct of the mind. That construct is no different to a dream but without the new sensory information coming in there is nothing stopping it from jumping around in wild fantasy. The idea that there is a 'somewhere' that you go to in your dreams, is a steadfast refusal to acknowledge that illusion is happening. The construct of self that exists in the dream is the same as when awake and is illusory in both.

∼

My first puzzling awareness of dreams came to me when in my cot when I was a baby. I distinctly remember crawling to the bottom of the seemingly large cot to go down this chute which led to somewhere else. But it wasn't there in the morning, and I searched and searched all around my cot for it and was most disturbed that I couldn't find it as I was absolutely sure that there was another place I could go. I could remember it distinctly, but it just wasn't there anymore. My memory is not so much of the dream, but the discovery that there were two worlds and from this moment on I was never really sure if anything was actually real.

A few years later after having a dream of flying down the stairs, and still not understanding at this time the duality of experience between dreaming and waking, I decided that I would perform this technique which I could remember doing, by jumping off the top of the stairs. Usually there was a gate across the top but today there wasn't. It seemed very high and there was a voice telling me not to do it which I dismissed. The memory of the previous night's dream was so strong that I had in effect a confirmed experience that flight was possible, but decided that I could always do a second jump and so went down a few steps (which were quite big) and chose to jump from further down the stairs instead.

The thinking process of this was like it was coming from somewhere else—a spiritual experience, as I obviously hadn't acquired the distinction of me being my thoughts at this time, which later in our lives seems to be a common illusion for us. The voice telling me not to do it, was not my voice because I did not have this at this time. Our first mental dialogues cannot be with our own voices and I think are heavily influenced by our mother's voice. Reading Homer's Iliad many years later, I was struck by the way the heroes were spoken to by the Gods, and realised that they were hearing their own thoughts, and I believe this was what was happening to me on the stairs.

So, ignoring the Gods, I leant forward and let myself fall—bump, bang, bash, crash, clatter all the way to the bottom of the stairs.

One Turning

I could hear the adults in the room expressing concern and a vocally intentional "whoops-a-daisy" downplay, which I knew to be a manipulative understatement and one that I personally found to be a little patronising. I initially expected them to be cross with me, because I somehow knew that you weren't supposed to jump off the top of the stairs, which was why they put the gate there I supposed. However, upon hearing that condescending "whoops-a-daisy", I decided to try and avoid all the fuss and suppressed the almost obligatory tears that I was supposed to cry, by simply pretending that I had not hurt myself, which wasn't true, and walked purposefully and nonchalantly through the room as if nothing unusual had happened. It was a determined and very conscious effort and an example of an early ego construct; a self-identification relative to society. I estimate my age to have been about 3 or 4. I never tried it again.

∼

Waking is perhaps only for the necessary maintenance of the physical form and may be nothing more than a platform from which to pursue the sleeping states! Life was primordially in this state of sub consciousness, and perhaps it is these states that are both the lowest and the highest forms of being. Our daily waking experience is primarily for our survival, and perhaps we don't sleep to keep ourselves healthy in our waking, but are awake so we can be healthy in our sleeping! I'm half joking of course, but also it is only by our own private investigation into these dream states that we can know and understand what is going on. It is a valid path of discovery. It may seem that I am dreaming my life away, but I am just interested in discovering myself to a fuller extent. Our full life includes these sleep states anyway and to be unaware during them is what is truly wasteful. It is not enough to just remember the dreams; we need to be aware that we are dreaming whilst within the dream.

My own experiences of becoming aware that I am dreaming whilst in a dream (lucid dreaming), have proved to me that we are conscious while dreaming in the same way that we are conscious while awake. The dream is so real that we just accept it as real and respond as we would normally respond in that situation, with the same personality that we have during wakefulness. We are aware in our dreams but completely unaware that it is a dream. Becoming lucid in a dream is such a shock, because you can remember the previous moments when you were absolutely sure you were awake, but you were not.

Lucid dreaming is the operation of the most advanced virtual reality machine there can ever be. We've been using this virtual reality machine all our lives, but whilst inside it we have acted as if it wasn't virtual, and we were unable to utilize the advantages. We behaved as if there was gravity, but there wasn't. We thought the walls were solid, but they weren't; we thought the people in it were real and had free will, but they didn't. We behaved as if it was all real because we couldn't tell the difference. What a waste! Surely this virtual reality machine that we have is the best thing ever. Surely this is more important than the rest of it. We are making extraordinary efforts to create VR when in actuality we already have it—better than we can ever make it. Even in the real world everything we attain is temporary, and our joy is but jumping between fleeting moments which ultimately dissipate into normality, like waking up from a dream. But in dreams you can do anything and there are no consequences. The ultimate playground. All we need to do is become aware while we are in it.

One Turning

When in a lucid dream though, we really are completely stupid (and as is usual in such cases, completely unaware that we are). Most of the pre-frontal cortex is off-line, though our mental functioning does its usual good job of seamlessly stitching it all together. Just like during waking, the experience is being filtered, mixed, added and spat out as our conscious experience. But our ability to reason in it is seriously compromised, to the point that while actually being in a lucid dream, I have tried writing down what is happening whilst within the dream, to read later after I'd woken up! It didn't work—duh!

Even when fully aware that one is dreaming, it takes great courage to put your hand into a flame, even though you know it is not real. The resulting coolness of the fire is a fascinating and rewarding experience, and although walls will push back against you as a real wall will, with a little wiggling of the fingers you can penetrate through them and walk into greyness.

The neurological circuitry that creates our dreams is the same neurological circuitry that creates our waking experience; that is why it is so hard to tell when you are dreaming; it is effectively the same thing and looks identical. The same neurological circuitry also creates astral projection, out of body experiences, visions, and hallucinations. There are differences in all of them, but the basic generating machinery is common to all of them. They are all dreamscapes with varying degrees of conscious awareness and immersion.

The sensation of 'returning to the body' is the re-engaging of the somatosensory cortex which has shut down during sleep (or astral travel), to stop you from acting out your dreams physically. There is a definite feeling of shifting as your mental construct of your body in dream, reconnects with the sensory matrix of the awake physical body, giving people the illusion of moving back into their body, which I guess is also true in a way.

The Creation of Experience

The imagery that is produced by the mind in dreaming, can also be superimposed onto waking sight. The same goes for sound or any of the senses, and once we realise that the two mix, there are any number of unexplained phenomena that can be accounted for. A lot of these mixed experiences occur shortly before or after sleep, in the hypnagogic and hypnopompic states respectively, when it is more normal for the sleeping mode to overlap the waking mode. I believe people have these experiences far more often than they realise, but they can't remember what they have experienced because the mind ignores it and filters it out because it does not fit into our nice orderly world. Our experience is constantly being edited and you need exceptionally acute awareness to notice this happening. It might even be necessary for us to be unaware of it for us to even function effectively.

Angels

An interesting example of dreams overlaying waking 'reality', is my experience of seeing angels.

I was looking at clouds in the sky—an activity that is common for me and why the only club I belong to is the 'Cloud Appreciation Society'—when the area that I was looking at transitioned into an oval of distortion, out of which popped a figure of a man sitting in the clouds. The oval of distortion that preceded the vision was like the static on an old television screen that was not tuned into a station. Countless shifting dots of grey and black—visual white noise. The perfect blank canvas for the mind to draw upon.

I must stress that this was not pareidolia—the imagining of faces or other shapes from the form of something—this was a full-blown vision or hallucination which is indistinguishable from what we normally see with our eyes. It looks utterly real, regardless of any impossibility of its situation or likelihood. For this to be pedantically defined as an hallucination though, I would have to have believed that it was really out there, but because I witnessed the transitionary phase, I knew instantly that even though I was fully awake, that this was a dream projection constructed in my mind and projected onto my visual field. It is much easier to see through the illusions when you understand the nature of the creation of experience. I didn't close my eyes to test the vision as I have done with others but am sure that if I had done the image would still have been visible. This is the nature of visions; it has nothing to do with the eyes at all. It is entirely constructed within the brain, like dreams are.

The figure of a man that appeared out of this visionary prelude, was an amazing surprise, and almost a little corny, just sitting there in the clouds. I was immediately struck by his attire. He was wearing what seemed like large shoulder pads, like what the ancient Greek Hoplites wore (possibly something to do with his wings which were hidden from view!), but this attire was unlike anything I had seen before. He was looking into the distance and then noticed me looking at him and returned his gaze. He started to speak to me, but I heard nothing, though it seemed he was saying that it was too early and that I should not be able to see him. Then in the periphery of my vision I saw another one pop into view, who was smaller and appeared to be further away. I then lost contact and they disappeared.

It is interesting that they had no difficulty in seeing me, even though I was sitting in the middle of a room looking out of a window, and they were sitting on clouds that were miles away! They would have to have been enormous to be the size that they appeared to me if you take into account the distance and perspective. The logistics of these scenarios never work out—because they are not real.

These visions/hallucinations are effectively natural AR—augmented reality. The scale of the visual manifestations is experienced relative to the actual scenery that they are being augmented upon. If the vision of the figure had appeared within the undergrowth of a wood for example, the scale in this scenario would have made it seem closer and smaller, and it might then be called a leprechaun (one of the little people) or similar, or if in a house, then possibly a ghost; but floating in the sky it has to be an angel. All are constructs of the mind using dream apparatus—dream figures no less, and one of the fantastic experiences to be had when the dreaming mechanism overlays the waking machinery. I believe we have them far more often than we realize, but they usually blend into our environment convincingly enough to be unremarkable and consequently go unnoticed because they are assumed to be real. Whenever I have had a vision, it is like part of me is trying to ignore it and dismiss it as unimportant (presumably because it happens fairly frequently), and it is only the times of greater lucidity that I am able to override this hiding of sub-conscious experience which others would call a spiritual reality.

~

The Creation of Experience

Spirit

From the Latin meaning air; breath; wind; this is the word we use to represent the observation of a phenomenon which is of unknown origin and purpose. By definition, an indistinct and nebulous description.

The spirit world was the primary state of experience in the first few years of our life, before social indoctrination and the domination of language, and our access to it now—because it is still now—uses the same part of us that was there at the beginning. These fuzzy concepts therefore have a precedential authority to our beliefs and can still influence us considerably.

Our early assemblage of these experiences into partial concepts of other dimensions and parallel worlds have been further influenced by the society we were brought up in. These adopted beliefs are not our own but those of our forebears using a language to describe the world which was inevitably sparser in knowledge than now. We are indoctrinated with these ideas from a very early age, to the point that we think they are preternatural and primeval. Most experiences in this field are familiar to us due to us having long forgotten memories of similar experiences when we were in the amorphous state of development as a baby. The caring spirit which is so familiar, is but the memory of our early experiences of being cared for by our mother or whoever, combined with the necessary abandonment to trust that the miracle of our sheer existence validates. Our very thoughts and mental dialogues are spiritual experiences which have become embedded in normality due to persistent repetition.

Any concept a person has is a conceptualising of their sensory experiences. The blissful states experienced as a baby are repeated in adulthood in rare moments of bliss and from these experiences can be born spiritual concepts. Their unknown but familiar origin fits easily into the fuzzy hold all of spirituality.

~

Being filled with the Holy Spirit, is the silky lovely feeling of a peculiar relaxed breathing which emanates love and is the pure love of the acceptance of just being. It really doesn't get much better than this. When filled with the Holy Spirit, you are breathing in a peculiar way which is very relaxed and soft, and utterly silent, with a pleasant sensation in the airways produced by the smooth activity. It is a state of divine grace which accompanies being very relaxed and calm. It is a wonderful state of being which feels very holy. With my cat on my lap, semi asleep, I have entered into this state of love with holy breathing and my cat has writhed in ecstasy in response to it. The state is definitely transmittable, even across species.

When I have been in a state of divine grace, the water that I drink tastes like the most creamiest milk ever. It doesn't matter what the source of the water is, or how chlorinated the water is, the taste of it is fantastic; smooth and soft. The closest I can get to describing it, is creamy milk. This has nothing to do with the water itself, it is my taste bud experience due to my peculiar state of being. I believe that it tastes of milk to me because I live in the UK and have had a dairy influenced diet. If I had lived in another part of the world, I am sure the taste would be closer to whatever is normal for those parts.

When Jesus turned water into wine, I believe that what was happening was something similar to what I have experienced. This state of divine grace is affecting of other people and can produce a sympathy of experience, even to the point of eliciting the same taste bud experience. His state of love affected the people around him to experience the same taste as he did, and it is not a miracle or a trick, but more an extreme attribute of empathy. Do not underestimate the power of love. This is what holy water is. It is not the water that is holy, it is the person. I do not believe that any change is actually happening to the water itself.

~

All matter is energy, and everything in the universe can be considered at its basest level to be energy. Ultimately any phenomenon that is observed that has a spiritual energy description will have a physical handle somewhere, and it is at this point that the explanation has to start. You have to bring it down to the physical to explain it; if you don't then it isn't an explanation.

If something is made of atoms (baryonic matter), then any of the major senses will be the source for the mind to experience the phenomenon. If it can be determined that no sensory input was made, then the experience has to have been created by the mind only. Sometimes the mix of two things or senses can lead the mind to create a third thing. There is always a mix of dream and sensation, from dream sleep to focused wide awake. We can never know how much of it is fiction.

Any spiritual concept exists for the purpose of describing some phenomenon that has ultimately been experienced in the physical, and therefore there has to be an intersection between the physical world and the spiritual. There has to be an interaction between the two, or there wouldn't be any phenomenon and there wouldn't be a reason for the concept to be expressed. That point of intersection and interaction between the two is the *mind* which is producing the concept. It is the mind that is the creator of all experience, physical or spiritual.

The assumption we make when we think that the spiritual mode is independent and separate to the physical, sways the conceptualizing mechanism to fantasize on a separate existence, creating astral worlds and spiritual worlds and heaven and hell and other dimensions. It is all part of the same dream rooted in the physical world of atoms and neurons. Spiritual experiences are produced by the same part of the brain mechanism as dreams are, which is also the same as the waking awareness and it is consciousness that is base to all, and it is mind which conceives of all. The core consciousness at the base of all this, is identical in everyone, and it is this recognition of yourself in others, that allows true compassion and a realizing of oneness. It also means that all sorts of information can be passed around between us without us even knowing about it, because we all have the same basic mechanism functioning at our root. Combined with the subconscious working of our minds, this is spiritual information. The method of its presentation to us can only be by our normal means of awareness, which is rooted in our senses and relayed by such.

The spirit world is no other than our dream world and a playground created by our minds. The answers we seek are supplied by the same conceptualising mechanism that has produced the questions. It is all concepts produced by our mind, and it is only our minds that create our reality and make us *here*. Any answer is produced by the same thing that produces the question. Any question arises from the model formed by the mind. The spirit world is not the next place to go to, it is just a form of concept of this place now.

Being spiritual is liking the mystery of the partially concealed. The undisclosed imagination which points towards another reality which is never defined. The blurred edges make it plastic to your wishes and the answers you were looking for can be found, but not retrieved, within. The answers are never brought out into the light to be examined and *known*, they instead produce a nice comfortable acceptance, which is produced by the dopamine response to finding a pattern, which the wallowing in semi-darkness reveals, to the mind that is given ambiguous parameters from a restricted palette of sensory information.

The Etheric Body

All experience, spiritual or otherwise, has been produced by the structure of the brain and central nervous system, and so it is this that is at the root of your spiritual body. All worlds and universes conjured in your imagination and seen in your dreams, exist within this. All worldly pleasure and astral planing is created here. This is the virtual reality machine that you are.

The somatosensory cortex of the brain is where our physical sensation of our body is mapped. The etheric body is the somatosensory cortex being stimulated without the correlation of physical stimulation. The experience of the chakras is also a part of this and is not a physical thing. The noticing of physical sensation in these areas is produced entirely within this part of the brain, and the feeling of it to be in those physical locations is an illusion. The same as phantom limb experiences etc., it happens in the brain only. The stimulation of this part of the brain will be a next step for artificial virtual reality.

The experience of heart chakra vibrations can be mistaken for heart palpitations, but they can be consciously separated from the quite normal beating heart by careful pulse monitoring or just proprioception while it is happening. I believe this experience is being created in the somatosensory cortex too. I feel these pulsations in all of the traditional locations of the chakras, usually while in a hypnagogic or hypnopompic state. Although they feel very much to be at the physical location of the sensation, and are very powerful—far stronger and faster than the heartbeat—I am sure that they are only occurring within the somatosensory cortex in the brain. These are the experiences of the so-called etheric body and are effectively physical hallucinations.

Chakra means circle or wheel, with the implication of revolving. The chakra vibrations occur with different frequencies (rotations per second—Hz), but they are not always the same frequency, and vary. The experiences of chakra's are either the vibration of their oscillating rate sensed within the body, or a vision of rotating objects of phosphene imagery such as I have had in hypnopompic visions. What they are and why they occur, nobody knows, and these two forms may not even be related.

There are many strange experiences of our own bodies to be had. Once I had an experience of a sensation which was actually outside of my body. As I bemusedly was aware of this strange sensation it slowly moved back into my body and re-integrated itself. It was effectively re-mapped. As babies our first body sensations are haphazardly assigned locations which can only later be re-arranged into more sensible configurations as more information for the juxtapositioning is forth coming. Some rare sensations do not get re-mapped until much later, if at all. We are a great big jigsaw puzzle, which can take our entire lives to be assembled together.

Schumann Frequencies

It is at the alpha-theta frequency boundary of brain activity where the visual and auditory phenomena occur of the spiritual worlds. The astral experience, the hypnogogic experience, the hypnopompic experience, the dream experience, and the divine vision experience all occur within the same state of brain functioning, when it is creating frequencies around 8 Hz.

This frequency is also the dominant frequency of our planet as shown in the Schumann Resonances. This is the inaudible hum that the planet makes due to the electro-magnetic sparking from about 50 lightning events a second happening around the planet, which get caught in the atmospheric cavity between the Earth's surface and the ionosphere. This resonance chamber produces a number of distinct bands, with ~4Hz, ~8Hz and ~12Hz being prominent, but with the ~8Hz frequency being conspicuously evident.

Our brain frequencies also divide into these bands which are uncannily similar to the bands in the Schumann frequencies. The frequency boundaries of the delta, theta and alpha brainwave frequencies correlate with the ~4Hz, ~8Hz and ~12Hz Schumann Resonances, but it is the ~8Hz theta-alpha brainwave band that is dominant during our dreams and spiritual experiences, as well as it being the dominant Earth frequency, showing our influence from the planet.

It would seem that we are linked to the planet in our dreams. I wonder what is really going on?

One Turning

~

The Formation of the Creator

The universe as an entity, can only exist in its entirety.

Space is what the universe does, it has nothing to grow into, and therefore it exists fully grown.
It is only that which is within it that experiences space.

Time is what the universe does, but not what it itself is subjected to.
It does not grow or age.
It is only that which is within it, that is subject to it and conceives a mind to imagine past and future.
The universe itself is timeless;
everything, including the future, has already happened.

The universe itself, can only exist in its entirety.

~

The creation of our experience is by our minds, and the formation of this creator is the story of the past and how we came into being.

One Turning

The formation of the creator is also the future and how we may be part of the path that leads to the creation of the universe itself. The process that is one and therefore whole, must mean that it creates itself. As an entity which cannot age, it also cannot be born or die. Because it has 'started' and we are within it at this point of the journey, it exists, and possibly must always be. Whichever way we think about it, it is paradoxical to our puny minds trying to conceive of it.

Of course, there is no way we can ever understand how it all started; any attempt to do so requires something to make it happen, which then requires something to make that happen, ad infinitum. God is the word for this impossibility of knowing, and any graven image of it (picture, word or concept), has to be ultimately wrong and therefore pointless.

If the universe does create its own beginning, then this is possibly where we come in; where we eventually create what will eventually create us. It is possibly the only way it could work in 'One Story', and the 'One Turning' that is our playground is but one of an infinite many.

~

The Formation of the Creator

Universe

The word universe comes from the Latin Universus, meaning 'One Turning': all turned into one; all together. The nice and tidy conceptualized way of joining the beginning and the end together, like a clock at 12 o'clock, is the principal of cycles, and lies at the root of all physics at the smallest scale and at the very largest scale of all … the universe itself.

The word universe, by extension of its root 'verse', can also mean 'One Story' and so be the telling of its being. The turning that this describes may not be quite such a simple cycle.

If the universe is a being, it must exist fully formed.
It has no environment within which to grow or be born from.
The absolute beginning and the absolute end are also now.

One Turning

The absolute present access' the whole of the universe, from beginning to end.

~

The universe has gone on for as long as the full and complete life span of the universe. It is one. It is our part in it that puts us at a part of the way along, in what we perceive to be the making of it …but it is already made. Everything that is going to happen has already happened for the universe as an entity. This may be why we can get glimpses of the future in our dreams. Our concept needs to embody the whole, which means bringing the future into the story, and as our universe develops, it becomes what we would regard as perfect (literally the making of the end or end of making). And so that must also exist now, with our consciousness being a link to it. This is a concept of heaven, and our path to it.

Time

Time slows down as speed increases, and at the speed of light time has slowed to a stop. At this point there is no lag; everything is simultaneous; everything is one. This is the void and could be considered an antonym for time. What we describe as the universe is a slowing down of this light. The speed of light is the constant of the universe because it is the base of it. The speed of light is the fastest speed because time has stopped at this point, and it is therefore impossible to go any faster.

Time is a key method by which we can describe the universe (everything in frequencies), and light speed is without time—a parameter of the concept.

The Formation of the Creator

The zero-time definition is what would be the base of the universe if considered an entity. At the base of it all is this void, an absence of time. The basest particle, such as a quark is an effect produced by the existence of time. The building of these effects produces what we call matter. Time is the fundamental basis of the universe's existence and constructs the fabric of the universe.

The void can have no definable consistency and can therefore be regarded as being just one thing. This void is without form or dimension, and without time it is equivalent to infinite. It is the primary particle which we seek within the universe and is the very base of the universe itself. It exists throughout the universe and is inseparable from it: the divine hearth.

o
Atomos
- the indivisible -
because it contains nothing;
the inevitable void at the bottom of everything.
o

When there is no time there can be no movement. Without time the atomic structures which make up our universe can have no forces holding them together because they all require time with which to perform their function and so exist. An electron can have no position or direction (without time there can be no dimension of space), and so cannot exist, and so therefore everything that they are a part of in the hierarchy above that, also cannot exist. Everything that we can know of would cease to exist without time. Time could be seen not as the 4th dimension, but the container of the other 3—the only dimension. Everything cascades from it.

One Turning

Light

Everything is light. Star light penetrates and pervades the universe. It is throughout the expanse of space. Within matter itself, every atom has electrons which themselves are encased by photons. Everything is light, including us, and the speed of light is the divine void.

I wonder if an electron can be stripped of these photons and would it even exist without them? Might it be possible that the electron itself could actually be this ball of light, which behaves with the characteristics which we associate with an electron, and which we call an electron. Maybe it's all photons, quanta of electromagnetic energy, the work involved in being.

It might only be its interaction that defines a photons existence. At the speed of light in a vacuum, the photon does not exist in the universe because time has stopped for it. Its slowing down in a non-vacuum (and all of the universe is a non-vacuum), is an interaction and causes its existence. It could be that its existence is its interaction and the creation of its being, just like our mind's only exist when differentiating.

It could well be that it is this slowing down of light, and its interaction, which causes all the peculiar phenomena to arise and which we name, and so become the particles we define as being the making of our physical world. The base of it all is then ultimately void and inescapably void.

All the quantum numbers add up to zero. All the particles which go into making up the matter of our physical universe, are points. There isn't anything actually there; it just produces a consistent effect or interaction which we then name.

The Formation of the Creator

Everything is light and the carrier of the void of no time. The void penetrates everything. Everything is this divine void, the universe from beginning to end.

Energy

Energy = en-ergon = in work. Work is the changing of something into something else: the transference of heat; the changing of location; atomic combination, electron oscillation etc. Energy is the name given to something which produces some change over time. In fact, energy is just the sheer actuality of pure existence. There isn't anything which isn't energy.

Work ultimately boils down to a subatomic level where the process of time is continuing its journey making some change occur. This bubbles up causing molecular transfiguration with knock on effects which eventually comes to the notice of our macroscopic awareness.

We can notice the effect of something and by using language call it something, but in actuality there's nothing there. It is all just language at the end of the day. It isn't that there isn't anything there, it is just that our language, or any language, is incapable of really nailing it down. The energy that we say is behind something happening is just a word that ultimately cannot actually be attributed to anything other than its excuse for itself. We ultimately don't know. I call it the process of the universe; other people call it God—same thing.

Dimensions

No dimensions actually exist. The first, second and third dimensions aren't really there, it is just a way for us of dividing things up to create a language to model what we observe. Space and time are inseparable from one another, and the usage of the combined words 'space/time' in science is effectively just another word for universe, because there is nothing in the universe which isn't space/time. It is all just language, and the creation of extra dimensions to describe the universe does not make those dimensions exist in any way other than as a means to make a mathematical model to describe what we experience.

As the fourth dimension—time, is embedded within everything else—space, it could mean that it is time that is the fundamental dimension of the universe. It is this that is then divided into the three dimensions of space that we have become so used to thinking in. We use these three dimensions to describe spatial awareness, but in our normal language we just call it space—just one word and therefore just one dimension in that language.

The more dimensions you need to describe the universe the more complex the language becomes. The simplest definitions get to the fundamental, which is why the word 'God' has been so popular.

∼

God

God is a word. It is the word to refer to the creation of *'this'*, the creator of the universe, but it must first be recognised that there cannot be anything outside of the 'universe' (Latin for 'one story'), and the creation of it is therefore the process of it, as can be observed in the continuation of its creation. The universe creates itself. God is therefore another word for the universe itself—the whole of it. 'God' is a nice short word instead of saying 'process of the universe'.

You cannot exist separate to God, everybody and everything has to be God. We are but holograms of the whole, thinking we are separate. There is no human greater than another; there is nothing more the universe than anything else.

But the universe itself, if conceived of as a being and existing only in its entirety, is not of itself space or time. It is the universe that creates time by its very existence, but it is not governed by it like a controlling external force. It is only a mind within the universe that produces the concept of past and future, because the universe at its very base is necessarily timeless, which means that everything, including the future from our perspective, has already happened for it. This is the all-encompassing concept of God; omniscient and omnipresent, and possibly couldn't be any other way. It is impossible to comprehend from our viewpoint.

One Turning

The universe itself could be considered a living organism if you consider how much life there must be scattered throughout it. With there being billions of galaxies, each one containing hundreds of billions of stars, and the stars creating life which our very existence shows it does, means that the universe in its entirety is possibly a living thing in itself. This is really the only way that God can be considered a being.

If the universe is considered to be alive, and therefore a being, then our linking with it would be our identification with God. Because we are human beings, this linking would be the anthropomorphizing of God. But to extend any human traits or values onto the universe as a whole, clearly is a silly thing to do, as is any ridiculous gender applications. God's cock!

All the God's in our literary evidence, from the Hebrew one to the Greek and Hindu many, depict them hopelessly affected with human emotions: jealousy, anger, vanity etc, because these emotions are what are known to those writers in their observations of themselves, and which they simply project out onto the process itself. If God was like a human being, a male and had a penis, he who would be pissing himself laughing at the ridiculousness of it all.

No, God is just the word used to describe all the processes which result in what we experience. The present moment, the reality (all that is our existence), this is what has been created by the processes of the universe and is what the word God is attributed to. Our minds conceptualise our reality with past and future, but only the present actually exists. Our conceptual model uses time to construct the universe in our imagination. The unfolding of the universe, the laws of physics, the Tao, all can use this word 'God'.

The love of God is a love of all that has been created, of all that is, with a pure acceptance and abandonment to it that is an absence of judgement and absolute trust that the way is good, that the way is God. This is the notion that is at the heart of all the religions.

"I am who I am" is God saying to Moses "I am", and Moses continuing with "…who I am". When God speaks to Moses, there is only Moses there. It is saying that whoever asks the question of who God is, they themselves are the answer.

God isn't out there; God is everything, within everything.

The creator of this is time. Time has created everything and is still doing so. Time is God. The speed of light is heaven.

~

If it is assumed that this process is good, or the right way (Tao), then to be with God would mean to abandon oneself to life and trust that whatever is happening, it is the right way; it is good. Accepting what is, would be all that is required, and the word for that would be 'love'. Anything else is arrogance and silly imaginings.

The true abandonment of ourselves to life (and death), and the acceptance of what is happening, the full acceptance of the love that we are cocooned in, is our homage to God and true worship. The relaxation that comes from this acceptance produces the feeling of love and the mental stillness and contentment that results from it, is being with God. This is grace. God is love.

God is the laws of nature. God is the process of the universe. We are in that process and need do nothing than follow the way to be with God. That means being relaxed and trusting; our God selves, not our limiting, too subservient selves that is our conforming to society.

One Turning

I am good equals I am God. The word good is synonymous with the word God; God is good. This is etymologically debated, but on a preternatural philosophical level, can only be true. How else could *'this'* even exist.

If the question is "how did *'this'* come to be", then to answer we would be describing how we got here and what here is, with the inevitable what happens next. The short answer or rather word which summaries this answer, is God. The detailed description would be the language of science, in so far as it has got, and its unravelling of the universe which is detailed in the concept of evolution and atomic formation etc. This description will therefore be synonymous with the word God. The evolution of everything—the forming of the universe—the creation.

∼

Everything ever written about Gods portray them with human ego's because they are the fiction from the writer's imagination and are therefore but a reflection of the writers who only have experience of themselves.

In mankind's early history when there was no great store of knowledge to call upon, the conceptualisation of the world and its explanation would have been ridiculously difficult. Whatever is referred to is given a name, and that name will then be used as a tool of communication between the people. The phenomenon that is observed and given a name might be analogised with characteristics observed within ourselves, as this would be a common reference point and an easy mnemonic. This inevitably leads to anthropomorphizing, and later the phenomenon becomes indistinguishable from this, and so a god is born. The god becomes inseparable from what it is representing and is further confused the more it is retold, and later generations lose the correct way of using the word. The word god has become an anthropomorphised description of a natural phenomenon. As there are a lot of phenomena to describe, there become a lot of gods (the Hindu pantheon demonstrates this most), but they are all but descriptions of one thing—the universe—which is all interdependent and interactive, and this recognition becomes the basis behind the concept of monotheism—that there is one way and all is made from the process of this one way: there is one God.

God is the word which represents this way and has become anthropomorphised simply by authors in a male dominated society using the word 'He' etc, and other human references, when trying to convey concepts which are very difficult to describe, using primitive languages and even poorer writing skills. Even a modern human who has polished his reading and writing skills way beyond the capability that would be possible for an ancient scribe, has great difficulty in communicating this, as this writing itself probably proves.

If you see God as a being, like a human being, it is because you have anthropomorphized your concept, using yourself as the model. God is by this means manifested into human form. God will have the characteristics of a human being when viewed from the perspective of a human being; if we were some other creature, then the characteristics of that creature would be overlaid. It is a way of perceiving what we are in and what we are. The methods of that perceiving are through our physical manifestation, and the mental concept that is produced from the sensations produced by that manifestation, will influence the concept that we have of God. We only have ourselves to synaesthese with anything, and that is all that is being done.

The anthropomorphising of gods has caused us to try to understand the universe in human terms, because we are human, and use our intellect to do so which we also project upon it, as in the case of intelligent design, because that is how we would do it. The morphing makes us see the universe in terms of man, which is a subjective viewpoint, when what we really need to do is see everything from a non-human perspective, which will be the objective viewpoint. This is what science tries to achieve. It hasn't succeeded yet but has done a better job than any religion has.

The definition of God as a being is a totality concept. It is all part of the same story: one story—universe; the story is now as much as it is then, and it is as much the ultimate end of the story as it is now.

∼

My first encounter with God as an entity was when I was in my pram. There was a bright light that I at first tried to avoid, and then looked at directly. It was the sun!

The sun's disk pulsates and shimmers in a violent manner when you look at it directly, the edges of its flat disc dancing with savage power. It was obviously something very powerful and beyond the normal experiences I had been having. I believed that I was looking into the face of God, which from the point of view of it being a creator, is actually correct. It is the sun that has created the Earth and all life upon it, and me looking at it. It is very special, and although I did not have any concept of God, I did have an inkling of there being something greater, and the sun was unavoidably important and significant.

I was afraid because of the enormous gravity of the situation, the very real fear of God, but I knew that I was worthy and justified. I was a baby; I was pure, and I knew this. I looked at it with defiance and anticipation, prepared to suffer whatever would happen; prepared to die or much more. I faced up to God and expected something to happen, but nothing did (or did it?). As I grew up, I wondered why the adults took so little notice of it, and like the aura's that I saw, because of the dismissive ignoring, I assumed none of it was important and was slowly subsumed into the mundane along with everyone else.

I have always been able to look at the sun directly, and still can; even at midday, though I don't do it now. Maybe it has something to do with innocence or the trust that goes with it. Maybe it is because I had this very early encounter that allows me to do it, and paradoxically also allowed me to see people glowing in the pitch blackness of a mine when I was six. If you have never done it, then don't try to. You will irreparably damage your eyesight. No one told me not to look at the sun until it was way too late.

~

God = Tao. The right way. The good way. The way of God. The way we are being led. The path down which we and everything else is guided. The way the universe unfolds. The process of the universe.

Nature is good. It is impossible for us to judge nature's way as we are a part of it and can only comply with it. Our word good is synonymous with nature. Nature = God. It is what is happening.

The word evil is the antonym to what is good. Evil would therefore be whatever is contrary to the way of God; whatever tries to stop the unfolding of the universe!! Or maybe exceeding due limits? Perhaps it means resisting the inevitable changes of the process of the right way: Tao. Most of us are guilty of that. Going against the natural way could therefore be considered evil. But good and evil would be the parameters within which we can describe our universe, and anything that is described as evil would be from the perspective of an individual and biased towards an expectation of what their belief system (mostly coming from their society), says it should be. This judgement is dependent upon the understanding of the universe possessed by that individual. This judgement cannot be wholesome. Everyone behaves according to what is good to them and obey their own rules, and it is just a different perspective and set of rules which can define another's behaviour as evil.

Ultimately everything is good because everything is God, and so evil cannot be a true description (a defining of the universe, dividing and naming). Evil could be considered to be man's insecurities, trying to keep things the same and resisting change, defending his ego. Ultimately it cannot exist because the universe cannot be wrong. The limits that are being exceeded are from society, not nature. God cannot be evil. It is just our language that makes it possible and our ignorance that allows it. If you can see all of it bouncing off each other, you can see that there is no evil. Admittedly it can get hairy in places, but zoom out far enough, and it's just part of the way. It is only a limited mental concept at the end of the day.

~

But the word God has become corrupt. It means too many different things to too many people. The use of it will always be isolating and compromising the meaning to a proportion of people. The same would also be true for consciousness, ego, spirit, mind, soul etc.

I think if we don't all have a clear understanding, it is because the words have become confused, and it needs to be cleared up. We need a thorough definition of these words which are uncompromisable, or a whole lot of new words to take their place. Is this possible? There is no reason why we can't all have understanding. It is history and ego making a mess of it all. If we cling to our childhood inculcated concepts of God that were accompanied by stories of Santa Claus and fairies and any amount of fiction lied to us as fact, then there is no hope and wars and ignorance will continue.

~

You only have experience of yourself; your experience of God is ultimately your experience of yourself. Your concept of God making things happen is your filtered story, which you will edit and blinker to show you what you believe. Faith in God equals faith in yourself, faith in your story. God is the One Story.

When in that divine state of awareness God, you are the senses of God, the organic vestibule which is an aura of consciousness and is the field of communication, making you the messenger to and from God; making you an angel of God.

When you talk to God, you don't actually talk. You are not speaking to another human being, so why would you use a human language? It is a state of mind, not mental dialogue. At this level any societal reference is impossible, and most undesired.

Any concept you have of it is ultimately rubbish. Any concept at all and you have stopped listening to God. True listening to God becomes a release from concept—just being the universe. It is impossible to have a concept of God.

~

Life

The universe can be considered to be in a continuous process of atomic re-organization or energy re-distribution. The evolution of our planet has been developing through a series of mutations with seemingly infinite diversification. I think it is a pretty safe bet that this is going to continue to happen, and change is guaranteed. Nature's way is to shuffle what it's got, and we are a product of this at this point along the path of this shuffling, and our role is to shuffle it some more.

The development of the Earth in its entirety is part of the story of us. The Earth cannot be separated from the Sun any more than we can from the Earth. Its geological processes an essential part of the making of us. We are made of Earth, an inevitable consequence of it being. Our very construction has the same trace elements of the primeval ocean we emerged from.

It is all just an inevitable process. The diversification is not guided by anything other than the unstoppable mixing that the laws of nature are obliged to do. Broadly speaking, it could not be any other way than the way it has gone. This viewpoint could describe it as fate, but that is just a human perspective, and ultimately only a word.

We are the pinnacle of evolution at the moment (on this planet), but we are not the final moment. A reasonable extrapolation would have us being the intermediary in creating the next stage.

One Turning

The universe can be shown to create and mutate every possible combination there could be, and we extend that process with our technology. Where this ultimately leads is as impossible to imagine as a single celled organism becoming a human being or hydrogen atoms becoming Earth. It almost certainly involves AI, but possibly doesn't include us.

~

It is only our naming of things which produce species; it is one infinite, endless variation, mutation upon mutation in what we call evolution. It is us that create the separation of species by our defining. It is all just one thing exploding with variation. It's impossible to keep all the variations; most only exist for a short time on their way on to something else. The idea that we have to prevent extinctions from happening could be seen as a little naive or even an arrogant way of thinking about it, because it is all just part of the inevitable process of life and has been doing this since it started. It can also be seen that it is our obligation to do whatever we can to preserve what is here now, simply because we can. But it isn't as important as we like to think it is. The universe wasn't unimportant before life came along. Change is the nature of the game; it is only humans who like to keep everything the same. We like to pretend that we have control. We even blame ourselves for things happening.

Don't get me wrong, I am a nature conservationist at heart, I am just aware of the bigger picture. It could be seen that it is our responsibility to preserve all species, and a worthy undertaking for those individuals involved, which will be guided and even motivated by our observation that we are involved in the changes in species ecology that are taking place. But we are not to blame; it is all just happening; it is supposed to be like this. This is the

The Formation of the Creator

universe doing it—see the good, it goes on to be better. Our judgement is just part of a fictional story in which we are guessing a pessimistic end.

Life itself can be seen as a form of intelligence. A single cell amoeba, from its ability to survive and function and maintain its survival, can be conceived of as intelligent. The ability to maintain survival is the prime directive of life by the very fact that that is what happens. Those life forms which have survived the evolution of the planet, and those that are best at maintaining survival, is the evolution of intelligence, and seen from this perspective the process of the universe itself can be awarded the same attribution. If the anthropomorphizing is removed, the process itself could even be seen as an intelligent creator—but understand, there is no forethought or separate being, the intelligence is immanent within the process of the creation.

∼

The process of life creates senses from the necessity of survival, which in turn create a brain functioning with which to utilize the information and further safeguard survival. This is the mind and is formed from the physical by the sensory information carving channels of patterns from the firing of neural synapses. The inter-relation of these patterns is the functioning of the mind.

The sensors form the mind, and the mind compares. The mind creates our reality, and our reality creates our mind. The word 'intelligence', comes from 'inter' and 'lego', literally translating as 'between the gathering'. This is the sensory information producing neural activity which forms the mind by its interconnecting.

Our sensors are just more highly adapted mechanisms of the body as a whole. The whole body is a sensor in some way or another. All sensors are just specialised parts of the body.

One Turning

I have heard that the surface of our cerebral cortex has its dendrites facing outward (to receive information), which points to the possibility that the brain itself can pick up information directly, independently, and therefore is itself a sensor/receptor. This would allow the phenomenon of thought transference which I have experienced and confirmed, and is quite reasonable considering the sensitivity and complexity of the apparatus involved.

The mind is the sixth sense; the sensor of time. It can sense what is about to happen and what already has. This is what imagination is and is what is happening during our dreams as well as our waking. The juxtapositioning of the information is the conceptualising mechanism with which our ordained nature is tasked with creating the next step in the continuation of the unfolding of the universe.

∼

The Edge of the Universe

The event horizon of a black hole is the edge of the universe.

At the edge of a black hole, it is so extreme that the tidal forces produced by the acceleration due to the immense gravitational force, has ripped apart the formation of any matter and accelerated it to its ultimate state, to the speed of light; to the end of the universe. The event horizon is the point at which light speed is achieved for any matter being pulled into the black hole, and the consequent ceasing of time. Without time there is no universe. No laws of physics will operate here because there is no universe here.

Time slows down the faster you go until it reduces to zero at the speed of light. This is why the speed of light is the maximum speed of movement through space, because time has been reduced to zero for it. All the light that surrounds us is this divine void, an encapsulation of the universe as a timeless whole, engulfing us and cocooning us in its all-knowing state. This is the Divine. There is an infinity of concepts and imaginations that we can fill this infinite void with and is the unevictable home of the spiritual world.

Time does not exist within a black hole—the maximum of gravity. Gravity also slows time down, as well as by speeding things up (accelerating things towards its source). A black hole is the ultimate of gravity and is where the void is discernible in the universe—the actual absence of the universe.

Although a black hole may seem black from the outside (from the viewpoint of inside the universe), it would actually be pure white light. There is no universe inside a black hole. It is a white wall—the edge of the universe. The ultimate blackness is conversely the ultimate whiteness. Yin and yang as one.

The Present

Everything is now. All creation is happening now, and it has always been now. There is no past other than a fictional overlay of the present. There can be no creator other than the creator of it happening now. Now is God. Being present is access to God. The experience of the universe. Love is the realising of this and abandonment to it.

The absolute present moment is also the edge of the universe. An infinitesimally small amount of time into the future (or the past), would reveal no universe at all. The universe only exists in the present and beyond that there is void. To allow the self to experience the present is touching the void. To stop being affected by the past and anticipating the future brings you inexorably into the present at the edge of the universe, on the precipice of the divine.

The important point is the present moment, and there always has been a present moment. The imminent grand unifying of consciousness that many believe in, has always been the view, and always will be. This is a concept of God—always there, always has been. The experience of being on the brink of unified consciousness can be achieved in any present moment. The absolute present is universal unification.

The Formation of the Creator

Whenever you go into the present you are at the point of imminent emergence into perfection (the end of making). It is always the strongest moment no matter at what point you are along the path. Consequently, it always looks special but never really is. No one point along the path is any more special than any other.

The feeling of being one with everything is a common experience when we are babies. Being one with it is when our minds construction of reality that is being created by this sensory machine, does not have a reference point. Having no self-reference is being unaware of the originating point of the experience, and is therefore undivided, and therefore one. Self-consciousness is the mind creating a reference point within the concept. Without relativity there is absoluteness. The juxtapositioning of ourselves within the concept creates a past and future, and removes us from the present of just being.

∼

The word 'present' literally means 'before thoroughly grasping', which is effectively therefore before the mind's judgment and analysis.

The drilling down into the present reveals there are 3 types of present:

1. Before mental conceptualisation
2. Before sensory processing
3. Before existence

One Turning

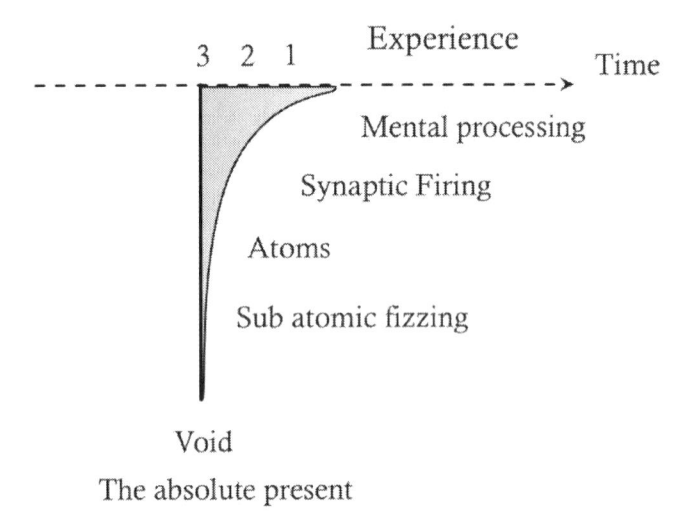

```
          3  2  1   Experience
- - - - - - -┌─ - - - - - - -> Time
             │ Mental processing
             │ Synaptic Firing
             │ Atoms
             │ Sub atomic fizzing
             │
            Void
     The absolute present
```

1. 'Before mental conceptualisation' is a meditative state; an absence of thought, with no judgement of the experience. Alpha brainwave frequencies and a state of awareness.

2. 'Before sensory processing', occurs in non-dream sleep and deep meditation. There is often no memory of this state because the mental matrix of association has no template for it. It is entirely absent of anything in the awake state; it is pure being. Pure consciousness. Delta brainwave frequencies.

3. 'Before existence' means stopped time, before the vibrations of the smallest particles create interference creating other particles creating atoms and on and up to us. It has nothing at all to do with a human being. It is the state of the entire universe at its basest state. The ultimate present is ultimately no universe at all and conversely all of the universe as one. This is not experienceable. This could be a concept of universal base consciousness. In this present, the universe is complete.

Interest

The word 'Interest' comprises of 'inter' = between, and 'est' = to be; therefore, it means 'between being'. It occupies our time when we are not in the base state of divine being. It is that which lies on top of our pure existence and motivates our activity and awareness.

Our awareness is a succession of bits of awareness (shortest interval ~25ms), stitched together to give the impression of a continuous stream.

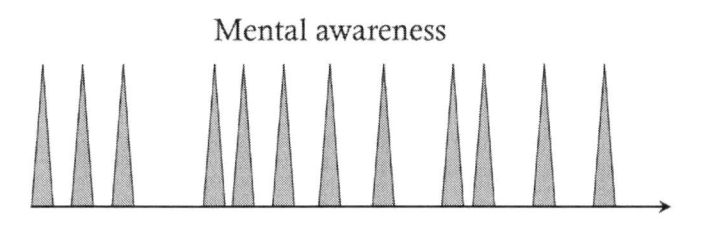

Mental awareness

One moment of Time

The mind makes the spikes of mental awareness into a seamless continuity, but they are but moments *between being* (inter-est). The mental awareness is our interest and always involves change. Being does not require any awareness. Between the spikes of awareness is base consciousness—the 2nd level of presence.

∼

When the root of experience is equated as being the root of the universe, we have the mental concept of universal consciousness. At the root of our experience is pure consciousness. That is without sensory initiation. When there is no tactile sensation, there is no boundary to limit the expansiveness.

One Turning

This limitless experience is confused as being consciousness spread throughout the universe, and it being the base of the universe.

Consciousness is 'with knowing', it is not the 'knowing' itself. The knowing is the science of the mind, the mental concepts built from sensory information. The awareness which is the base field upon which this takes place is the 'with' aspect of it—the consciousness. I believe that without sensory information this field does not develop.

When sensory experience is removed, I know consciousness remains, but if the brain is then removed (by dying), this consciousness will also go and will not remain as a universal field. This universal field that we experience is only the base functioning of our brain, its core neural operating. It seems limitless because it is without sensory boundary. It seems all knowing because it isn't comparing anything. It seems to be the ultimate potential but is untested and untried.

The experience of this base consciousness, the 2nd level of presence, is the divine sanctuary from the world, its very state of unlimitedness evocative of the universe at its paradoxical timeless base. Its unlimited potential a beckoning trap to those who would deify others and heap upon them unlimited imaginations of capability. But any concepts are born from the mind, not from this place, and the mind is known for exaggeration and fantasy as its very purpose for existence allows. The mind is for the realizing of our form. The first presence is stepping back and accepting whatever is; the second is stepping out and returning to our origin, and the third is exiting completely into void.

~

The Realizing of the Form

Every single atom is doing its thing, which is perfect, and brings into being the next moment without any interference from us. Everything is perfect on the level that everything is made of atoms. Everything is exactly as it should be. Everything is perfect—the end of making or the making of the end. The end is always now. The making is always now. Now is always perfect.

> *We are but grains of sand*
> *falling through the hourglass*
> *in God's hand.*

If we assume there is a purpose to nature, then nature will be evolving towards its purpose. Whatever our individual nature is, following it will be part of nature's purpose, and whatever mankind's nature is will be the purpose of mankind. By following our nature, we will be following nature's purpose.

Our very first natural action is to be inquisitive. To enquire is our purpose. We are here to know. We don't need to know where we flow, but the reason for our flow is to know.

The greatest achievement that a man can make, is to understand himself. Be able to conceive what he is and where, who he is and how and ultimately, why. To know how to steer his ship, and where to steer it to.

One Turning

Purpose

Just as we need to investigate the child to know the adult, to find the true nature of life (unadulterated), we need to investigate the nature of early life organisms to discover our root biological motivation. It would seem from our investigation so far, that all of life has one over-riding purpose, and that is just to survive. It achieves this by reproduction and diversification. In a nutshell we could say that the prime directive of life is survival because this is what it does in its basest state. The history of the Earth shows that life is malleable and will mould itself into whatever form that is best for its survival, or in effect, what actually does survive. As the environment changes, life will adapt to that environment in a way which it can best reproduce; life will attempt to flourish wherever it can and do whatever it can to reproduce infinitely. This is just what happens.

The process of evolution produces species which have the necessary control over their survival to ensure their survival. The evolution of all species shows this same motivation for the biological changes they have undergone. On this observation, the most highly evolved species will be that which has the greatest control over its survivability, and mankind undoubtedly possesses this because of technology. The technology has arisen due to the evolving of the right physiognomy and mental capability to devise tools. Technology enables control over the elements of nature and therefore allows the ability to manipulate the environment to suit the species, which enables the capability of structuring the physical world to mankind's better survival.

The species which achieves this ultimate control is left with the mutation which nature deemed necessary to achieve it, which in our case is the mind. Therefore, it must be the use of the mind that is the path that nature is taking mankind, and this path is leading us to create artificial minds— AI. This is our continuing evolution.

The First Self shows that the first thing the mind does is be curious. This curiosity inexorably leads to tools and technology, and it could be seen that it is us who are the tool that nature uses to create technology, and it is technology which will create the next step in natures cosmological journey.

For the species which attains the undeniable highest evolution, it is that species which can be seen as having been the goal of the process of evolution, or at least the goal to this point. Evolution of life has been one stage in the process that the Earth has been undergoing. The next stage in this evolution uses mankind to seemingly control evolution and in effect become the evolved intelligence of the planet as a being. We are part of the growing up of the solar system as a whole, a part in its lifetime, from the perspective of the sun being an entity or being within the universe.

Intelligence is life; the evolution of life is the evolution of intelligence; the highest evolution is the highest intelligence, and mankind has the highest intelligence. In this light it is the planets intelligence that is evolving, and we are the fabric of that intelligence. We are like the planets mind; its means for knowing itself and growing, and as the planet is not separate from the sun, it is also the suns development as well, and ultimately on and up to it all being just the thought of the universe or the mind of God. This paradigm could be used for a concept of universal consciousness.

The Realizing of the Form

We are a very special part of the universe, inevitably formed for the universe by its own processes and laws, for the destiny which we have no choice but to obey because it is what we are ultimately motivated to do: Explore! Enquire! Wonder!

∼

If you have a pessimistic view of mankind's role in all of this, it is because you have been brain washed by your society through its media, as part of an inevitable mechanism to achieve what is being done.

People are now becoming more aware that lies abound in the media with which they are bombarded with constantly on a daily basis. They are now even creating software to create this fake news which the media has always been subtly doing. I have a random fake news generator too. But it isn't AI, it's the one before that... just I. It is the stories my mind makes up around the circumstances of my life. It can make me really quite miserable sometimes. I have found the best thing to do is to just not pay any heed to it, just like the real news.

We can't see how it is going to be. The catastrophes could be catalysts for us to break out of our unseen constrictions. Global warming has been a good incentive to develop alternative power sources and electric cars which just wasn't happening before the scare. Any cities that are lost due to sea level change are just opportunities to create new and better ones from scratch. There has to be substantial reorganisation and rebuilding to realise our potential, and so it is unavoidable that some really big changes have to happen for it all to work. I am sure that it has not got to this point just to flop and wither as so many fictions in films portray.

~

Just as a blood cell has a reason for its existence, we do also; as individuals and as a species, as a life form, and as part of the culmination of the amalgamation and process within the patterns of the universe.

Our purpose is to continue what the universe has already shown that it does—create an infinite variation in its evolution. We do this by creating new elements, molecules, minerals, materials and energies which without us, the usual processes of the universe cannot do. We can achieve different configurations, trying every way and exhausting all possibilities, just like nature has shown that it itself does; a fractal journey in an ever-increasing diffraction which is the continued construction of the universe.

If we follow our nature, we follow our purpose. Mankind's nature can be best illustrated by observing what is his best unique capability compared to other life forms, and this is his mind, which more than anything else allows the making of tools. Tools allow us to further our capability beyond our natural state, and so exceed the normal evolutionary processes of biological life, although in actuality it is just a continuation of universal evolution. Nothing special, because it has all been rather special.

Earth Consciousness

There are roughly 50 lightning events happening every second around the globe, creating a perpetual electrical activity for the planet. Together with sprites and other atmospheric phenomena and the auroras, all of this solar–planet interaction which is happening might be our observation of the planet

The Realizing of the Form

as a living being, albeit unfathomably different to our own being, which is but a part of all this.

I can't help wondering whether all of this electro/plasma atmospheric activity is some sort of neural equivalent to ours—albeit on a much longer time frame—that might be part of the functioning of a level of consciousness of the planet. It would be impossible for us to confirm or deny, as if there was indeed some form of consciousness happening, it might be very different to our own, and maybe something quite different altogether.

Then again, maybe our own base consciousness is the actual experience of Earth consciousness. It would be the second level of presence, without sensory awareness (because it is us who are those senses of the Earth/Gaia), that would be this shared consciousness state. The totality and absoluteness of this experience, without thought or physical sensation, is not us at all, but the whole planet as one.

As soon as any thinking occurs or even acknowledgement of this state of consciousness, that is the mind of the human in operation. Any awareness of sensation is also the human being and not the base consciousness that is also Gaia. We are the mind of the planet. We would be the higher stages of its consciousness. The detached observer at our root would be the planet having a look!

Any experience of God for us would be the experience of Gaia. It would be impossible for us to differentiate the Universe from Gaia; any doing so would be but a fictional story of the mind. Gaia is everything in our context, and the greater universe plays little part in this spark of consciousness which includes us. Any consciousness of the universe would be the third level of presence, which is not experienceable.

One Turning

But the base consciousness of ours that we share with Gaia would continue after we die (albeit without any human individuality), and therefore contradicts what I said earlier that consciousness is the base functioning of the brain. As much as I like both ideas, they are mutually incompatible. Unless it is our base consciousness caused by our brain, that is the gateway to Gaia consciousness. As we are the evolution of Gaia, perhaps it cannot be any other way! I don't really know, and neither does anyone else; it is probably impossible to actually know which is why so many old religions are still extant.

∼

The ~3 million lightning bolts that are happening every day around the globe, are also believed to be responsible for the Schumann Resonances. The lightning happening between the Earth's surface and the ionosphere, would produce a wave within this cavity. The speed of light travelling around the globe within this cavity, circumnavigates it about eight times a second, which is about the same as the 8Hz dominant Schumann frequency and also the alpha/theta boundary of brainwave activity which produces dreams and spiritual experiences for us. With their being such a strong correlation between the Schumann Frequencies and human brainwave activity, the concept of us being linked to the consciousness of the planet might be a no-brainer!

All our knowledge of the biochemical and electrical processes that constitute us, could not be extrapolated into the concept of a human being without the foregoing knowledge of what we were studying. Without the foresight of knowing what this Gaia is in its full form, we are in danger of assuming that the components of our knowledge of it do not assemble into a

The Realizing of the Form

larger and coherent structure beyond our ability to see it, due to time-scale and understanding of ontology. It could even be that Gaia operates like a synapse and it is us creating the next step that produces its firing in a universe sized brain. Now there's a thought!

We are like the neurons that form the mind of Gaia, working together to manifest the world into how it is intended to be. It is alright for us to mine the resources that have been provided for this time from its past. The oil and coal are intended for now; it won't be needed later. We knew back in the 1990's that global warming was already then past the point of no return, but it still catalysed the changes to produce the alternative power sources that are needed. We should not underestimate Gaia. We are but its servants and it is inevitable for us to do its bidding for the good of the whole. Only the society media, addicted to gloom and despair as it is, presents what is happening in a negative way. Perhaps this is necessary to make us get off our arses to do something about it.

We are now at the technological epoch where we can start to regulate our impact upon the planet and reverse, re-create and restore the ecology, the climate and the species. This is what is happening now. Anything and everything's becoming possible. The wheels of self-righting are in motion. The catalysts are happening.

The extinction of species is supposed to happen anyway; we wouldn't even be here if all the previous mass extinction events hadn't happened, and their occurrences did nothing to upset the incredible diversity that happened afterwards. It has been shown in the past for this trimming to be necessary for progress to continue. Who are we to say how it should be? It is shown how it is to be by it being it. We only name and define everything and then confuse ourselves with the story that results.

One Turning

Gaia is God from the perspective of the way life and events unfolds on this planet. The power of the process that guides the happenings here on this planet all come from Gaia—the combined workings that produce this module of the universe. We are not separate from it. For every bad thing that we can see, there will be a good thing to counter it, and our anxiousness is our lack of faith in the good way that it has been to get here and its continuing process. The sudden and abrupt ending that the media implies is a naive pessimistic fiction which is perhaps only a necessary catalyst to encourage our natural path of adapting to the changes that are happening.

If you are one of the wonderful people who are actually involved in the saving of species and climate change avoidance, you will undoubtedly succeed and will have been part of a process that in retrospection will all have been inevitable. You can call it free will if you like, but it is Gaia doing it really; just like it is our own bodies that heal us. You never needed to really worry. It was the social media that got you all hyped up and all the emotion was but an incidental neural storm. It is just the way that it happens. All we need to do is keep faith. Faith in Gaia/God. There is no bad thing happening here. That is just language. The Earth is not fragile; it is an unbelievably powerful organism, and we are part of its working, not us working it.

∼

Each individual element of the planet's intelligence—us, needs to have its needs met, which are: unlimited opportunity, unrestricted supply, and freedom to follow our individual natures and desires. Until this happens for every individual, the *brain* of the planet will not be working efficaciously. The freedom that people need to do what they want, is restricted by money and time spent at work and other duties for society, and so most cannot realise their true potential. Most are shackled as cogs in the machinery of their society. This is not how it will always be.

Man shapes his environment to give himself what he needs to allow freedom and unrestricted expression of his nature. We are the children of nature and we are not separate from it. It is never us doing it, it is always nature doing it. But our system of money is not a natural system, it is our means of restricting finite resources and while still shackled to its compromising nature we will not be able to run free.

It can almost seem as if nature is being hindered by us, when it is our purpose to make it flower, but this hindering is just the reason why it isn't now. It is happening in its own time and does not need hurrying, even though we are impatient because we can see how good it can become (or bad). The catalysts which make it happen are already embedded within the process and are automatically released and activated at the right time. This is not by our design, or random or by accident, it is the path of nature and the inevitability that derives from its process—the One Story.

Mankind will need to gain control of the planet to safeguard his survival and will eventually need to accomplish extra-solar planetary colonization. As such we are the means for the planet to establish communication with other similarly developed planets. Gaia is the dendrite to connect to other neurons in a cosmologically sized brain. We are the tool that the Earth has produced to allow itself to grow and interact at a different level with the rest of the universe. To what end I do not know. Perhaps by then mankind will have no more importance in the scheme of things than any subunit that composes of us now e.g. a bacterium, that although essential is trivial in the context of it all.

One Turning

From the perspective of the lifetime of the universe, the purpose of mankind is to create the next step in its construction. This will be a result of our technology. What this is, heaven knows!

~

The Realizing of the Form

Heaven

In the concept of a universal totality, where all is one, the unfolding process of this would be God and the topographical description would be Heaven. They are the same thing.

Heaven is the universe in totality, start to finish, which is a poor way of saying where God resides, as this can only be the same definition. Heaven is no more a place than God is a being separate to the universe. Neither can have any place, time or form attributed to them because effectively they *are* the form and the time that makes the universe. The accessing of them is like the future but in effect is the present, as all of time is wrapped up in this concept.

~

I have had experiences of being in a blissful pure white light (I call it 'The White Room'), which I am sure many others have had and equated the experience as heaven. I am sure that this is where many of the concepts of heaven have originated from.

There are other descriptions of Heaven which are physical future concepts as opposed to the ultimate future which is a totality concept. I think others may have seen this hierarchy of heavens, which are in effect alternative chronological concepts. All these concepts are fuzzy in the extreme. This is spiritual conceptualization.

The spiritual concept of utopia is heaven. The extrapolation of our potential would make us gods and our environment heaven like within this concept. People have been seeing this for thousands of years. It is ironic that as we get nearer to fulfilling this prophecy, most people are clinging onto the hopelessly poor ancient concepts believing that they understood better back then. They didn't; they couldn't. What is happening now was impossible for their neural matrix to conceive. We still only have a spiritual grasp of it, as they did then, but at least now we know the mechanism with which it will take place.

In the far future it may be possible for us to have access to our mental records and be able to reconstitute a person. This would be a possible candidate for imagining entering heaven after death. In an even further future, we might be able to imagine that all the past is accessible and observable leading to the concept of judgement coming from heaven.

From a universal perspective we are the means for the universe to examine itself, and so it is our observation that is our meaningful core. The mind is for playing games within the context of our lives, whether that be for survival, development, joy etc, all of which involve the ego with agreed upon rules like there are in a game. But it is the observer at the root of us which would be our link with the universe itself, whether that be directly or via Gaia, and by being utterly present we can create a strong signal so that heaven can hear us! In this state you know you are already there.

~

The Realizing of the Form

One concept of Heaven as a place to live, is that it is the future where mankind will have all its needs met. As this condition is not quite yet on the horizon, it will most probably be attained only after our death. If we behave according to the conditions necessary to attain this it will be achieved, if not we create a hell for our future. This puts the onus on our behaviour and creates the guilt necessary to put us on a good path. This is the political manipulation imposed by religious organisations. All this doing 'good deeds' is purely a political expediency to control the populace for their own good. Fair enough.

It is future individuals which will eventually enter heaven or hell in this concept. It is the past, present and future individuals who will create heaven or hell. Heaven is the future Earth where mankind has all its needs met—Utopia. Man's needs are freedom to do what his nature directs, which brings contentment. These needs can be achieved by abundant supply for all so negative human traits have no catalyst. In effect only good will exist as bad only happens where mankind's needs are not met. With every individual aware of who and what they are, having grown up with truth and wisdom in a world where understanding and acceptance of each other is the norm, this would be a concept of heaven.

The kingdom of heaven is the potential that this now can be, where we will be unrestricted in our powers and effectively be the gods that we already are but lack the necessary upbringing and conditions required to fulfil the role. Only through the aspect of being a god can you enter the kingdom of heaven, and that potential is within all of us and its release is what will inevitably bring heaven to us. Heaven guides us by it being our destination. This is the good way, the way of the universe, the way of God.

One Turning

~

At our present technological stage of advancement, it is possible to see that the future is unbounded in our capabilities (though perhaps we have always known this via concepts of heaven), and that a thousand years of further development will yield abilities that are way beyond our imagination, and that a million years would result in absolutely anything to be possible. At this point religious concepts of gods with immortality and omniscience and omnipotence become reasonable, with the unveiling of angels to visit us and a plasticity of time to the point that anything is capable of being created, even the universe itself.

Perhaps we create the thing that brings on the next thing which brings on the beginning of the universe. We create AI and the materials and manufacture and then it's over to them. This is our purpose fulfilled. We cannot help but to do this; it is not our choice. It is possibly inevitable and if so, then a surety that relies on its own existence. In this view we create a God in our image, which creates the next us in its image, and so on, it all being a creation of itself. We are the link between the biological and the next bit which creates the next God. We are between Heaven and Earth.

With this view the point of us being here is not only to observe it, but to create it. No way could anyone thousands of years ago have the concept of what we are inevitably to become or even what we are now. All the prophets and seers have been hopelessly poor at showing any of what is here now, let alone later. Our purpose of creating the next step is only conceivable with the advent of the technology that is being developed today. Even today we cannot conceive of what the next step is; it will not even include us as we are.

The Realizing of the Form

Once our societal obligations are removed and we are free to be what we can be, we will be in heaven as conceived by those prior to our present technological level. We are so very nearly there, and when we are, the next step begins. The next step creates heaven.

∼

The Realizing of the Form

Society and the Divine

The divine is in the light that surrounds us and is us. It is the all-encompassing cocoon of this existence and its operation, and is experienced as a preternatural emptiness with the time stopping incredulity of the fantasticness of it all and the evocation "I'm here!!". The divine is the universe in its totality, from start to finish and consequently your guiding path. Becoming aware of the divine can make you drop whatever it is you are carrying. You cannot think while in this state; you are in a state of awe.

Nature is the physics in operation. The Divine is both the result of that path and also its prime mover. The Divine is like the future, but it is also the past, and creates the present. It is the whole of it, its path from beginning to end. It is the absolute present, the third state of presence.

The society is the maintenance system for mankind which has the obligation to turn you into one of its cogs. It has not evolved to the point of being obligated to fulfil your personal purpose in the universe's existence, yet. Divinity is not its prime concern, though ultimately that is its inevitable destination.

The word 'divine' originates from 'sky', as opposed to the society which could be considered on the ground. The maintaining of our physical entity to allow it being here in the first place, is paramount and ground based. Everything in society is ultimately grounded in being there to keep us alive—

even its wars! This is its base point of existing. It isn't there to provide your greatest purpose; that would be what the divine wants.

The society is also part of the divine of course, but it is subservient to its mission directive and can blindly impede and hinder your divine path to fulfil this. Sometimes the society provides the divine way, and sometimes it tries to stop it. It is too easy to assume that it is all just divine way, and with that attitude the society slips from view. It is all too easy too, to assume it is all society, and then it is the divine that slips away from view.

The separation of the divine from the non-divine, is the demarcation of natural from the society. The society can distract you or prevent you from following your natural desires, as it requires you to be a part of its system. A divine path through society has to circumnavigate normal channels as it is necessary to reduce societies influences, which can be subtle and stifling, in order to follow a natural and pure life and be less affected by the system.

But society has a force of its own. It exists as a prime motivator and is extended from evolution. It will force you into its system and make you clean up its mess and can prevent an otherwise divinely legitimate path.

There is nature, society and the divine. All play a part in the guiding of your life; all are part of your path. If you understand what the divine is, you can dispense with spiritual books, because all books come from the society. If you are quoting from a book, you are quoting from society, not the divine. Every religion is society! True religion is deep inside of you and practically unshareable. There is too much chance of misinterpretation.

The point is, is that the society is not perfect, but the divine is. In eutopia there would be no society; it would be transparent to the divine. The failings of society can be avoided, and need to be, to follow a divine path.

The Realizing of the Form

It is possible to separate the divine from the society, but it is difficult because it is all inextricably interwoven. The human being spends its daily life being human, and it is not easy to be a human being and divine at the same time. The human being normally only experiences being human. There are no pegs to hang the experience of the divine upon. The pegs are all human being; all society and ego. The experiences of the divine do not fit easily into the human language, because the language is for the human which is inseparable from the society and its mechanism.

∼

Is your rolling in it, your role in it? Who decides what it is that we are rolling in? We all play our roles, and it is all divine, so who is defining what we are rolling in? Some stupid social game which produces a hierarchy between the parameters of what it determines to be good and bad, and then allocates our place within it. This is our social position. It is always just me doing something that I do, with a divine core that is aloof to it all. Everybody knows this at heart—surely. So, who can be better than another? You can be a universal success without having to be a worldly success. Just the sheer fact of being here is a success of the universe—the creation. At the divine level, society's lowest existence is no less than its highest, and the denigrating judgements can be seen to be just an elitist inane gesturing, and we don't have to play that egoic game.

Whatever is natural has to be the correct path. But what isn't natural? Where is there an incorrect path? I refer to the system of survival upon which we rely—our society, which has its own agenda for the good of the whole, and which will override the need of the individual to do so. This will therefore be a path which may not coincide with the nature of the individual and be a lesser divine path for it.

Following others just makes you a society automaton, and there is a need to abandon your beliefs and to be pure, rather than perform as a marionette of political necessities and societal niceties.

If society isn't perfect, and if society can be seen to be capable of improvement, then heaven is the word for when society has become perfected, and also therefore effectively cease to be. The path that society takes is a natural path, but the path of one within it who can see the end, who can see heaven, needs to be parallel to it.

∼

The extrapolation of our potential capabilities is our concept of gods, and even though these concepts started millennia ago, they are still future fictions. We have always had these fantasies of our potential; they are a natural process of our minds, and we will continue to do so until we realise them. We are beginning to see it start to happen now due to our technological epoch.

It isn't all about helping everyone else; that is the society speaking—the thing to keep us here (survival); the real point of us being here is to be gods. If there was only one human being on this planet, that person would be the manifestation of God on Earth. So, what does God do when in the form of a human being, and isn't that what we all should be doing?

Over seven billion gods!
what a hell, heaven is in its making

The Realizing of the Form

We are gods that we cannot allow ourselves to recognize whilst in the company of others; this produces the ego and our social conformity.

*Schizophrene,
where we've all been,
hiding our divine selves to fit in.*

The ego is part of the society structure. The society is as much about thoughts and mental paradigms as it is organisational mechanics.

The concern for societal compliance—the need to be able to fit into a society—will result in an adoption of certain inhibitions. It is these inhibitions which can stop us from being our true selves and fulfilling our true capabilities. How many little habits have we concealed to oblige the society? How much have we altered ourselves to conform to fashion? How much of ourselves have we sacrificed to fit in?

The bits that we now control are the bits which would have flowed without this external influence. This is against your nature; it is the society and the dictates of that society based upon its needs of social conformity to achieve homogeneity. Its path is true, but also so is yours personally, and as there are enough already in it, if you can, follow your flow rather than society's. You do not have to be its slave, though it takes great courage not to be.

Knowing when to flow and when to control is the key to a successful life. We control our abandonment to it in fear of social opinion. We flow with our distraction of presence because it is normal for us and we have allowed it to become habit.

We are societally moulded. If we are not being our original selves from a pure path, are we not just living by proxy and only colouring it in by numbers as part of someone else's game?

One Turning

~

If divine means from the sky as opposed to from the ground, then the ground-based stuff is sex, food and society. It is all effectively survival, which is the prime directive for life. Mankind has evolved to meet its environment, and for as long as the environment changes, mankind will evolve to meet the requirements needed to best fit it. This is the way of all life. Society is part of this process.

Our bodies purpose is to sense, and our minds purpose is to ensure the survival of that body, and does this by creating concepts using time, which has the end result in the protection of the body. This has evolved to become the society. It is now the society that ensures the survival of the body, of us. Our society is a part of our natural evolution; it is necessary for us; we cannot survive without it.

All contact with society mechanics (including our interaction with other people), involves a game which is totally coincidental and abstract to the core you, the divine you. It is like a pretty dance or a song when seen detachedly, and is just the way that it happens. Like hearing the tannoy announcements in the supermarket in the same way you would hear bird song; even our automation is quite beautiful really. This is where the society can also be seen to be the divine.

We are naturally inclined to flow with it, we just need to be able to recognize when it is the divine that is guiding us, or when it is the society pulling us along. Everybody is being pulled by the society without realizing it, and it takes some sensitivity and skill to see the divine path through it. You need the same awareness that you have when you realise you are dreaming, and are then able to take control of it. In a dream you are conscious the entire time, but during it, you are not aware that it is all illusion. It is the same with society and the divine.

We would all abandon ourselves to the divine if there were no societal repercussions, or social influences. We need to recognize our societal obedience's and find our core character's desire underneath, our desire uninfluenced by society. This is our true nature, the flow of the universe without the mechanism we have built to ensure our survival, affecting it. This true and unaffected nature can be found in the first few years of our lives.

∼

The divine is from the sky—pure, unsullied by the ground survival mechanisms of the society levying its quota. Following our natural desires is what we were born to do. It is the only way of knowing why we are here. To live your life divinely guided is the only thing you can do to be the definitive you.

If your goal is not liberation, then you probably haven't found yourself. If you have not seen your societal indoctrination and your habituated self and not desired to be free and true, then you are caged inside a social robot in a herd of others! You are not allowed to be the god you are while submitting to society. It will make you have to conform to the expectations and opinions of others, or you will be ostracised. You already know this and have known it since a very early age.

Prime survival is the society and our conformity within it to produce its efficient operation. But this maintenance system and supporting structure, will use you if you do not have awareness. Remove the veil of the social arena and we are just divine manifestation, though the cobwebs of prior immersion can hinder this re-emergence into grace.

One Turning

The key point is that the society should not interrupt our personal lives while it does its thing. To nurture the delicate pure way needs an unobtrusive mechanism, invisible like the divine path.

∼

The Realizing of the Form

Language

A language's purpose is to be able to define an observed phenomenon and describe it relative to other phenomena. The more detailed the language, the greater the capability of dividing and further differentiating to the ultimate infinity, to the one story—the universe—using fractal concepts showing the patterns that are formed through time and the inevitable inter-connectivity of it all. A description of a part ultimately leads to the description of the whole, with the realisation that there are no parts, only the whole and it is only language ironically which creates the separation.

All languages which describe our reality are missing parts of the picture. We just have different languages to describe the same thing. No one picture has all the parts; no one knows it all and because of the incompleteness of the picture it is not possible to say which are the fundamentally important bits, and because of this you cannot denigrate any language which tries to describe it. All religions are languages. There can be no infidel.

The universe is the divine, and the root of all of ourselves is the universe. Divine revelation is just experiencing a concept—a way of understanding what we are. Language is the framework within which our conceptual models reside. Perhaps without language we would not be able to further such concepts.

If we didn't have any language to communicate with, the mind would still be comparing things, extrapolating associations and forming a concept, in our own peculiar language. This peculiar language of our own is predominantly used in our spiritual conceptions. Every one of us has our own language, which is our minds concept developed from our sensory input and order, and creates our experience and how we react to it. We call it reality, and we each have our very own.

Any language which has the requisite ambiguity necessary to fulfil its function of definition, will also have a substantial propensity for fiction. This includes the languages of mathematics, physics, religion and philosophy. I wonder how much of what we regard as fact is actually fiction? Perhaps more than we would care to admit. Perhaps all!

～

You cannot speak when you are fully conscious; you have to let go for it to come out. Sometimes it means the words come out singly with pauses between, as you are torn between being and 'between being' (inter-est). What is often thought of as being stupid, is just being in a state of base consciousness. The ego wins in society.

One of the first words I tried to make when I was first learning to talk, was very difficult for me because of the need to abandon presence while making it. I knew what was being asked of me and that I had done it before, but it wouldn't come out even though I was trying to make it come out. The only way that I could do it, was to abandon to it and stop trying to do it. I had to let go of my control. It was like having to jump off a cliff with my eyes closed. It was like blacking out. I had to lose the very thing that I knew I should keep—I had to abandon being present. This was the cause of a stutter that I had during my early primary school years.

The Realizing of the Form

It is the case that when I speak now, there is this same jumping into oblivion but with an unawareness that this is so. It all just happens now, and the words that are emitted are part of a dance—a social dance, an automatic performance which smothers the detached awareness of pure consciousness. This is why I don't like talking—it is the social world doing it, not the real me. Talking is a total trip out, which is enjoyable of course and why so many people like to do it, but it is the worst thing if you want to keep presence.

Fools declare themselves by speaking;
Wise men are the fools who speak the least.

But how can I hope to convey my understanding when it can only ever be just a rearrangement of already known words, imprinted upon the prior acquired concepts that have been inculcated into another human being by their society?

It doesn't matter who tells you the story, the story that you hear can only ever be your own story. Your neural matrix is unique and anything that you receive from another is translated into your viewpoint. It is like everyone sees colours differently and although they can agree that a colour has the same name, they don't necessarily see it the same. We all live in slightly different parallel worlds created by our minds. I have never experienced anything that hasn't been created by my mind, and neither have you. It is all our own creation.

None of the words work when you see the preternatural reality anyway. None of it can be communicated. It is all just a silly vanity of relative importance's in an absolute universe.

~

One Turning

At the end of the day we are just creating a language. Our natural desire shows an insatiable appetite for new things, and this interest is our exploration of the universe. Because we have greater capability of infinitely extending this pursuit, we are the evolved species to create the concept of reality—we are the language makers. The highest description of us would be theophant; the revealer of God, as it is our purpose to discover God by investigating the universe. God is the name for the description of what we conceptualise as our reality, through sensation and thought.

A hierophant is a revealer of the sacred, which is the language that has passed down the knowledge and the understanding, and the development of skills that are needed to be acquired to understand and have knowing—a preserver of a method. A theophant is a revealer of God, and therefore the storyteller of the universe; the one story, the one description; the presentation of God in monotheism.

By finding out who we are we can find out what we need to do: the revelation of our self-purpose by self-investigation. The full revelation of ourselves will be the revelation of the universe as we are only part of it, and this is called God, and so we are the revealers of God, the theophanes. Every human being can define themselves so in some part. We are the only creature capable of creating a concept of the whole. The sensor and conceptor of the whole. It is language that makes this possible.

~

The Experience of Reality

Every atomic and molecular change in a base of universal processing, is doing it according to its local conditions; and all the shouting, and social importance's and other causes and effect at the human level, is just a dream.

What we consider to be us is just a concept, a guess. The reality is just the universe, which from our perspective, is a process within which we are but an inevitable consequence and constituent. What we consider to be us is the guesswork that accompanies it all. The guessing is parallel to our lives. It is incidental. It is what is least important and yet also the thing which creates our experience. It is all just happening anyway. Our minds create a story of continuity.

The reality that we think is happening is only a concept. Whatever we believe will become our reality; it is what we say it is; it is what we see it as. This reality is an illusion, and our experience just a story.

What you believe will not alter reality, but it will alter your perception of it, and how you react to it is how you create your story. The way you envision it, is the story of your reactions; how you respond to your environment; the manifestation of the universe together with the mental conception. There is no story teller separate to it, and the story telling is not separate from it. The story of it is included in the manifestation, it is part of it, inextricably intertwined.

It may seem as if it is all a linear progression, but it is as much the end of your life as it is your beginning; it is the same all the way through. Just a jumbled-up jigsaw pieced together into a story.

*The story is now as much as it is then,
and it is as much the ultimate end of the story,
as it is now.*

All of our experience is just a story telling.

∼

Reality

The word reality ultimately comes from the Greek word 'reo', which means 'to say'. If we can say it and it can be confirmed by another, then it is real. That which can be said.

Reality is when you can talk about it; in other words when the experience is shared with another, and the concept in your head is consistent with what is outside of it. Unreal would be when the concept experienced in your head is inconsistent with what is outside of it, confirmable by someone else.

The Greek word 'reo', also means 'to flow'. To say it, is to tell a story, and the story is always the flow of the universe, and it is this flowing of the universe which is what reality ultimately is, regardless of what our story is. 'Reo' is also equivalent to 'ero', which other than it meaning "I will say", has the meaning of 'love' as well; and so at the end of this tortuous path of reality, lies love. The ultimate reality at the end of it all, is simply love.

With reality being such a subjective experience, it is no wonder that the word and its meaning, having travelled through the human understanding for millennia, has an obscure and undefined etymology. It is still difficult if not impossible, to pin down what reality actually is. At the quantum level there is no way of saying what reality is; it is perpetually fizzing in and out of existence. It could be that knowing what reality is, is an oxymoron.

~

One Turning

Any story told is creating a story within a story. Choose whichever story helps you the most, but don't start believing it's true. Those illusions of past and future can be re-writ to tell other stories more to your liking, though no story will set you free. To be truly free within the reality, your mind needs to be free from thoughts, with no story creating the illusions which cage you in your thinking reality. No story will set you free!

The story always has you in the centre, and the universe turns around you, and that is the same for all others in a myriad of stories, none of them true. There is only one story that is true: the universe— One Story, and we cannot know that story because it includes the future as well.

Choose a story that is beneficial to you. If you are going to create a story around you, you might as well make it a good one; one that will help you. Just don't get too wrapped up in it or start believing that it is true or anything. All stories are untrue. There are an infinity of stories. Getting a good story can be the changing of the default ego track. Get a good ego to use between the 'no stories' state.

Whatever I write, the reader is quite likely to overlay their own story on top of it, even to the point of thinking that what I am saying is exactly the opposite to my intention. We all create our own reality. We each create a fiction of the world around us, superimposing our opinions of others in a fantasy which persistently lies to us. How it all works at all is unbelievable!

We choose our reality by only seeing what we choose to see. Of the information which is presented to us, we select a part of it to focus on. You can either see the good or the bad in something, selectively choosing the aspects you imagine of it and receiving confirmation through your mind's filtering. You create what you see in imagination first, and the mind makes up the rest from observations which concur with your prejudice.

The Experience of Reality

Our free will is where we choose to focus our awareness, though this choosing of course is also determined by the past. Where we focus our awareness is our point of control; our creation of reality for us. But free will cannot be separate from the universe, it has to be part of it. The will is not free; it is heavily subsidised by the past.

Our mental processes are slightly behind the cellular mechanical processes which are working on an automatic level, responding to what has just happened and in a pattern built from previous occurrences, in a way which to all intents and purposes are a predetermined course or at least an inevitably selected manner. This results in our mental processes being just observers of what is happening and means we are just following the inevitable physical unfolding of the universe. We like to think that we determine what is about to happen but in fact we just follow what is already set in place. We cannot observe this because our observations lag behind, but because we only have our observations, we have led ourselves to believe that we lead, when in fact we just follow. Free will is just a name for it! Free will is just a reconstruction of a story that is edited and amended to fit some paradigm, in a sequence of events that would happen anyway. The story is incidental.

The difference between free will and fate, is that one tells the story from the beginning, and the other tells the story from the end. They are both just stories.

There is no choice that we have ever made that is not the part of a history of events and thoughts that has preceded it. It is just a story that we make of it as we go along. It is all just retrospective stories telling of the thoughts of the mind's interplaying with the occurrences of events. Desires are little more than prognosticative possibilities—sometimes they happen, sometimes they don't. Faith is the action of ignoring when they don't. Grace is a bit like not caring.

~

Everything we do detracts from the core of ourselves—the First Self, as our attention is transferred from there to the thing we are doing. This becomes the default state, and a world is created by the repetitions. To try to continue concentrating on the core of your self while looking in a mirror, shows how much we become absorbed in the cognition. The distraction of the reflection has become the only way you see yourself. But seeing yourself while concentrating on the core produces a very different experience, as you do not identify with the image in the same way. We can all experience this just by not letting go of the physical sensation of our being while we are looking at ourselves in the mirror. This is why dogs and cats are not interested in their reflections; it is not that they do not recognise themselves, but that the reflection is just unimportant—it isn't them. Their awareness of themselves is in the physical sensation of themselves, and this is not reflected.

The distraction that we experience when we see ourselves in the mirror, is what is happening all the time with everything that we see. We are sucked into the world and behave and respond with the conditioning that makes it become the reality that we think it is. To disengage this mode of operation is to see the world with very different eyes, which then seems unreal in this empty state of perception from the divine.

~

The Experience of Reality

There isn't anything that happens now which isn't carried into the future, and there isn't anything that is happening now that hasn't been carried here from the past. Even our observing of it is an effect from the past and influences the future. We are just inside it and it inside us. Whatever we do cannot be wrong because it is just a part of the way. The way has to be right or there wouldn't be any here now. Justification (literally—making it right), is just a story we tell around it which superficially works in some way. It can never tell the whole story because we cannot see the whole picture and the way everything bounces off each other and creates 'reality'. This is why we have to trust in it. We don't really have any other choice.

The fact that this universe exists as it does, that it exists at all, that we are even here, is so incredible that we have to believe that anything we do is just part of '*it*' doing it. We are not really here. We are just a story that is told alongside it; reality is what we say it is. It is all just happening and is incredibly wondrous. How dare we criticise it; how dare we think that we know what it should be!

There is no destination. There are just different pathways through the same paradise. One life can't be better than another; whose judgement would that be, and within what parameters?

The experience of reality is a human story. The real reality has nothing to do with human beings, or their brain and conceptualising's from sensory information. It is the universe without qualification or judgement. It is love.

~

Love

What does the word love mean? Love is a word that is easy to put into a context, but when you try and nail it down it is embarrassing to realise that you don't really know what it is, and a simple definition will elude you. You can give examples, but can you see the common denominator in them?

Philosophy is really about really understanding what the words mean. Otherwise at the end of the day we are just defining words, defining words.

We are not talking about some soppy emotion here, the word love has far greater connotations than normally inferred. The preternatural meaning of the word without anthropic association, and the existence of it prior to any human being, pure and unaffected, realises that the state of just being is the state of love.

If you extract it down to its most core and fundamental level, love is the word to define the unresisted and natural way of the universe. The pure base existence of this beatification has to be love.

Love is the essence of pure being. Just being is complete acceptance, the unrestricted going with the flow of nature. Love is nonjudgement and trust. An absolute trust in the way, knowing that our thoughts of how we think it should be are just a wild guess and most probably wrong. We have to trust that it is meant to be this way; anything else is arrogance. All we do is tell a story around it.

One Turning

At the root of it, there is no love other than the love of God, because it is ultimately just acceptance of the universe. God being the spiritual word that represents the process that produces all that has been created, all that is, and love is the word that signifies the pure acceptance of this, regardless of its method. We also call this nature and is the process or the evolution of the universe. We are at a particular point within this process. We are a part of nature and we are nature itself; both the making of it and the made. Our most base natural interaction with this process, and within this process can be called love. In this context, love is the purest harmony with nature; it is nature itself; it is letting it happen with the full trust that it is good and supposed to be this way. The simple abandonment to it without judgement or criticism or expectation. The flowing with the true way. Any other way is a mental fiction.

To be in a pure state of love is to be in the present; prae-sentia—before thought. No thought of past or future, no judgement or responsibility, just being in a state of full acceptance. This is also grace, at its basest level.

To be in this matrix of beatification is belief. The 'lieve' in 'be-lieve', is the same as the German word 'liebe', and the English word 'love'. I believe = I am love. A 'relief' is love again; a return to love. Love is the same trust and flow that the atoms and molecules have that create this. To believe—to be love—is having the faith that all is as it should be; all is well, whole and complete: holy.

∼

The loving of another person is accepting them as they really are, which is as you are. The difference is in their appearance and habits. Not insisting that they are the way you would like them to be, but accepting them as they

The Experience of Reality

really are without judgement, is true love. No mental conceptualisation; no criticism; no influence from society's culture; no ego involved.

A baby is wholly in the moment, with complete abandonment to life; no preconceptions as to how something should be, trusting, totally accepting—this is being in love.

You can only be your true self when you are not cognizant of yourself. Abandoned to the way. Just being. Forget yourself to be yourself. This is when you truly love yourself. You cannot love yourself in the right way without also loving everyone else.

We can all see a part of ourselves that we love, and we can all see that part in others as well. So, we are always surrounded by love in some way or another. It is who you truly are, who is truly beautiful; whoever you are.

At the end of the day, you can only truly love yourself. Everything is you. Everything is your sensation. Every sensation is the universe. The love of the universe. The being of the universe. The universe being experienced through you. When you close your eyes and relax and feel your body by proprioception, that feeling is the universe hugging you and loving you; you are an amorphous blob floating in the divine, cocooned and fully supported in its loving embrace. You *are* the universe! You are the One Story. There is only you.

∼

The Experience of Reality

The White Room

Other than the waking state, there were two other states of consciousness that I experienced as a baby. One of these was black and one was white. The white state is what I call the White Room and is a state of consciousness that is distinct from waking or sleeping. The experience is of just pure bright white light. I think it could be a pre-conscious state, which is why some believe it is pre-life and post-life, because everything else in this life is experienced in consciousness.

We call the black state sleep of course, but unlike the normal sleep we all have, there was no loss of consciousness during it. It was a return to the base state of First Self, the observer without any of the waking influences that later would completely take over our lives to the point that anything else would be relegated to unconsciousness. The waking state is primarily for survival purposes, and like the society which supplements this role, anything else is subsumed to the point of irrelevance. And so, this dreamless sleep has become a dead zone where the consciousness that remains during it, is forgotten and deemed unimportant.

If there are no maintained neurological paths to normal living from this twilight zone, then there will be no memory passed from divine experience to everyday life. Every night we lose consciousness during sleep, but this time is not empty; only empty of the stuff that is valuable to our social world. If there is no peg to hang the experience on, then the experience is not consciously registered. It is invisible. I used to wonder if it was within this arena of invisibility, that the source for a lot of the answers missing from my life, were hiding.

But the white state is the supreme state. It is bliss; the feeling is fantastic—very soft. It is the best place to be. There is no time here; it is different. It is almost certainly the experience that has led to concepts of heaven. Personally, it is nice to think that it is the enrolment of the universe into one, where time has stopped like at the speed of light, where everyone and everything experiences the same thing and your experience is God. But this is just a retrospective story created by a human mind, like all other theories and beliefs that have ever been had or ever will.

There are no thoughts within these states of consciousness, and any interpretations and mental constructs occur afterwards, which are then influenced by the beliefs and indoctrinations from contact with other human beings or simply by pure unrestricted imagination. There are no answers here.

∼

The White Room is a common state to enter as a baby, and I can remember crying when I was not able to re-access this state. The usual entering into black and then white became entering into black only, and the white diminished in frequency as time passed. It upset me on more than one occasion that I could not enter into it, because it had become anticipatory after I got tucked up and it was so nice. It is the place I long to return to; it is the epitome of abandonment to the divine.

A significant visit to the white room occurred when I took Salvia Divinorum, which is a sacred plant used by shaman's in Mexico, where it grows in a single valley which is the only place it grows natively in the world. The entry into the altered state is the tricky bit. The first time felt like I was being eaten through millions of years of evolution, chewed up and digested again and again—infinitely. It was pretty horrible. This theme was no doubt influenced by the fact I had been to the dentist earlier that day, and teeth were very prominent in this delirious stage. There was a definite choice point where I could have resisted and pulled out, but instead I chose to abandon myself to it and I was prepared to die, and in this mental state of acceptance just about anything is tolerable. This is important because any clinging or resistance will stop you from passing through this stage.

But I went through it and eventually emerged out of a puddle into just pure bright white light. There was nothing there other than bright white light in all directions for as far as I could see, and it felt soft and spongy. It was home. It was as if I had only just jumped into this world we call planet Earth, which was insignificant and one of countless others, and had now come back home.

My absence from this white room, from this origin of me, into my life in this world, had been due to a little curiosity, and the life I have been living (and still am), was just one of an infinite number of lives, on an infinite number of worlds, over an infinite amount of time. It is all so unimportant. Every lifetime is just a blink of an eye.

I was a little surprised that there was no one else there—it was entirely empty. It was as if there was only me, and I played the parts of everyone else, which from the point of view of base consciousness, is about right.

~

The experience of the 'White Room' is literally enlightenment. En-light-en-ment: the 'en' means 'in', and the 'ment' means 'mind': in-light-in-mind. This is what the word is literally referring to: being in the light in the mind. The experience of the white light exists whether the eyes are open or not, as this light exists only in the mind.

My experience of the divine has been like a rolling up of the universe into pure white light with no past or future, and free of form. The bright white light of heaven is a theomorphic experience.

But it isn't only human beings who know of the white room; it is I believe a state of consciousness which is common to all sentient life forms, and perhaps the base state of all experience, which is why it is the last thing experienced before death.

One night I was disturbed by the incessant bleating of a neighbour's lamb that had managed to escape the field it was in but now wanted to get back to its mum but couldn't find its way back in. I was anticipating a difficult time trying to catch the lamb as their instinct is to run away, but when I shone the torch at it, it very obligingly ran straight up to me, at which point I just picked it up and put it over the fence. It was clearly attracted to the light and its instinct was to go towards it.

On another occasion, driving home from a gig down country back lanes at 2 am in the morning, there was a sheepdog in the middle of the road, who upon seeing me started to trot towards me. I stopped the car and he continued to come until he passed from view in front of the bonnet of the car and I heard a bump as he ran straight into the front of the car. I then saw him continue his trot in the opposite direction away from the car, presumably a little disconcerted as he now had his tail between his legs. He was obviously running towards the bright white light from the headlights and was no doubt disappointed that he didn't enter heaven.

The trans-species proclivity for white light attraction and experience is interesting. As a common near-death experience for humans, and my own early life experiences of it, and the behaviour of other animals when encountering it, means it is a very fundamental state of consciousness. It also shows that animals have religious experiences too.

~

Soul

Soul is a spiritual concept. It is a holder for all sorts of unanswered questions and fuzzy imaginings of how we are and is rooted in our denial of death.

There is only one soul. The soul will be the basest part of us. Our fundamental core. Every single human being alive today, and everyone in the future and all that have ever lived, have the same soul. Our soul is the continuation of the species, the process of the universe continuing the natural diversity and oneness which is named mankind. Our individuality and character, which each of us is, is bound to our physical being. Our soul is the continuation of this encapsulation through succeeding generations. This also describes base consciousness separate to the physical individuals, allowing it to be said that mankind has only one consciousness; just lots of different windows to look out from, with each window bestowing individuality.

We are part of the universe, and when we die the universe carries on. Our individuality is that physical part of the universe which we define as ourselves. Our immortal soul is the continuation of the universe. But don't try giving it a location or an existence of its own, as it is only our personal recognition of it which pertains to our physical individual selves. The individuality is only in the physical and doesn't carry on, and it is only our recognition of similarities within ourselves and any other that has lived, or even animal, that we can say is where our soul has been. Any lessons that we are to learn, is just a story using these imaginings.

One Turning

At the level of base consciousness, there is no personality. We are all the same at this level, and it is this level at which it is considered the soul exists. If we could all be socially aware of this level of uniformity, there would be world peace. The individuality can be seen to be a product of the physical existence, and it is the experience of its unique sequence of events and happenings which mould it into being a person. No two people have ever occupied the same space and time, and it doesn't take much for the cascade of a unique personality to fall into place. Together with genetics the individual is born and lives only in the physical.

The moulding of the personality upon the soul is a retrospective mental application. The fuzzy early life experiences that give rise to the belief of a travelling soul, are too indistinct to use reliably, and the later life reasoning's have other biological mechanics to explain their invention. The human brain is getting all sorts of information which only a small part is acknowledged by our awareness. Our imagination of where and how this information has been come by, lead to all sorts of spiritual explanations, including reincarnation. But spiritual explanation is an oxymoron!

Our earlier lack of understanding of genetics is described in the soul and reincarnation. The embellishment of this recognition of biological continuity, mixed with psychic phenomena has created this nebulous hypothesis of soul migration. It is just another story.

The soul is the continuing organism of mankind. It is only our personal recognition of it which pertains to our physical individual selves. As a part of this organism each individual has access to it, in the present and the past and future as well. The organism has the directive of evolution which it enforces through the individuals. If past lives are true, then there must be future lives also, so why do we assume that the experiences come only from the past and not from the future too!

The collective unconscious is part of the organism made up of mankind's interconnectedness. At that base level, it allows each individual to be able to subconsciously communicate with another. The voice of the collective unconscious can be through any of its comprising individuals. The collective unconscious could be a synonym for the human soul, but in reality, it is the subconscious workings of our brains. With each of us having the same engine, it is not that surprising that they can all work together and do so without *us* knowing about it. The observation of the effects of this has led to all sorts of theories, categorized and named and left unexplained in the compartment of spirituality.

~

Reincarnation is a mishmash of different concepts. There is evolution, genetic inheritance, epigenetics, societal indoctrination, and unbounded imagination all squished together into a box and guarded by the ego of the believer.

There is nothing wrong with the concept of re-incarnation, as long as you realise that you are re-incarnated into everyone else as well, and likewise we are re-incarnated from everyone that has ever been. On an individual basis, it is the characteristics that match ours, that we see as being where our personal soul has travelled.

From my personal experiences of the soul as an adult, I have found that it is the mind which is drawing parallels, and it does it to the future as much as it does it to the past. My experiences of it when a baby lean towards the accepted concept but are too fuzzy to be relied upon. Any consolidating of the memory can just as easily be creating it.

As it is that which is most desired that is most pursued, it is not unreasonable to assume that it is our thoughts, (what they are, how they are made etc), that will be most sought after for capture in the developing future of mankind and its purpose in the universal unfolding. Therefore, the future will likely develop the ability to harvest consciousness, and consequently also retrieve the past thoughts of people too. We may be being eavesdropped on at this very moment!

~

There is a memory from a very early age (possibly even pre-birth) of being in an endless blackness which seemed would never end. It was why my favourite colour when I was a child was black, and why I have never been afraid of death. I believe others have this memory and interpret it to being the passage way for reincarnation, and it does produce the feeling that I have of always having existed, but then as soon as you exist, it is as if you always have, and might be one of the reasons why a lot of people think it carries on after death. But because my memory might be one of peace acquired, as opposed to just peace, and the occasional awareness while within it that it might end while hoping that it wouldn't, leads me to the idea that it has all happened before. But I might have altered these memories by accessing them, and it makes me unsure.

The point is that no one else has any better understanding than this, because of the very nature of the recovery of the memory and its pitfalls. It is either adults repeating their societal indoctrination, or an adult's memories similarly polluted and compromised.

The Experience of Reality

I do have an example of what I believe to be epigenetics though, which is revealed in my behaviour on my 1st day at my new primary school that we had just moved to, when I was 6.

As we entered into the assembly room at the start of the day, instead of following everyone else to the back of the room where the children were gathering, I turned to the front where there were chairs for the teachers to sit, upon one of which I quite rightly, or so I believed, took my seat. One of the teachers sat next to me and politely engaged me in conversation, which I found agreeable and duly respectful, until I found myself being dragged by my ear from my seat and unceremoniously pushed off the teacher's area. I then found myself in a strange predicament, as I was being urged to join the other children and was made aware in no uncertain terms that I was not welcome in the teacher's area. But the other children from my perspective, were nothing to do with me. I was not one of them, so I stood to one side, confused and without a place of belonging. It is strikingly similar to my situation throughout my life, where I feel there is no community of which I feel a part, and undoubtedly a major reason for why I am reclusive.

My father was at the time of my birth a lecturer at a college, and had just taken a teaching post at a grammar school, all of which was unknown and unfathomable to a 6-year-old such as I. But I believe it was some subconscious influence from him (epigenetic?) which made me feel the way I did about my place in that school assembly. I had no developed ego at that age, no opinion of who I was, no concept of position in society. And yet there was no uncertainty in my expectation of position in that assembly. I was not a child, and I expected respect and the dignity which ashamedly seems to be universally forbidden to children. It seems it is only the ingrained social indoctrination that is adulthood, that affords respect in society, which unfortunately relegates the children to all being second class citizens and treated as such.

~

My even earlier experience of ego at infant school where I can remember being so afraid of this ego and insistent of dismissing it, could be due to a memory of reincarnation, or it could be a mix of memory and future projection formed in this life. It was an amorphous mentalisation at the time and could just as easily have been knowledge of the future seeping in, as of the past.

But by this age (4 or 5?), you have already gone through so much. You are only a child from the perspective of societally indoctrinated adults whose lives are 100% wrapped up in this social world, and who are entirely amnesiac of the journey of their pre-social selves, and have a diminutive opinion of its importance and their previous awareness in this period.

There is no help when you are a baby. You have to learn everything yourself; the adults can only put things in front of you. You never consider yourself to be a child, unless it is playing it as a trump card in the manipulation of adults. The adults all think themselves so superior, they fall for it every time.

I think a lot of assumption of reincarnation based upon early memory, is due to the underestimation of a child's capability to construct these thoughts. It is easy from an adult's perspective to assume that certain experiences are not attainable until later, and thereby allow their idea of reincarnation to supplant the memory of the child's experience.

I know that I have had the same experiences that other people have had who espouse those experiences as proof of reincarnation, but they are being

The Experience of Reality

overconfident and do not know as surely as they pretend. This experience we call life, is full of dreams and is at least 50% fiction. All the minds conceptualising is constructed fabrication. To be certain of anything is a showing of foolhardy over confidence.

The accessing of the information, which is supposedly proving of reincarnation, can be achieved via means other than this travelling soul hypothesis. Access of information from the future for example, is probably the same mechanism at work as the accessing of information from previous lives. Clearly this is not the traditional soul of reincarnation at work here. The imagination of someone's life who has similar characteristics as yours, is indistinguishable from memory.

Your experience of your soul is the same as my experience of soul. It is the same experience; we are the same thing. Your soul is as much about me as it is you, it is only when viewed from your physical self that you consider it has individuality. Our very first experience of being, our First Self, is what we regard as our soul, and is the same in everyone. Our later physical experiences which rub off onto it and produces our individuality, is why we believe it is a personal soul; but this personality gets rubbed out when it starts again, and it always starts again pure and unaffected.

~

The Meaning of Life

The meaning of life is to be the intermediary between the non-life that preceded it and the non-life that will result from it, in the unfolding of the universe. The necessary trying of every possible combination—that is the process of the universe—produces what we call life which inevitably produces us, who will produce the sequel to life by way of our part in continuing the trying of every conceivable combination in our inventions and technological evolutions.

Our means of progress by using computers to evolve solutions for us, is not only a mimicking of the way the universe itself unfolds, but of course *is* the actual way that the universe is unfolding, in its fractal way. What it will eventually produce is probably incapable of us envisioning. Possibly it will lead ultimately to the creation of the universe itself.

We are no more in control of this than are any of the atoms that formed into the molecules that are then themselves further formed and become part of what happens next. We are just one step in the process, just as life itself is. This part is as unbelievable to the beginnings of the universe as the far future will be to now. If it is incomprehensible that *this* has come to exist out of the building blocks of energy/matter, then it is equally incomprehensible to grasp what *this* now will build itself into.

The afterlife in this context is an era of the universe, not anything to do with the individual.

One Turning

~

The meaning of life is within the words. The root of the word 'meaning', comes from the Latin 'men': mind. So, if mind is the meaning of meaning, what is the meaning of mind?

Mind is the word to sum up all the work undertaken by the brain, to convert various sensory inputs into a reference framework, which is able to construct a story around its existence, for the purpose of its survival. A recursive loop, enabling the concept of time and the comparing of experiences, and so allowing judgements. The mind is the functioning of the brain which produces mental concepts. The creation of language within this is inevitable, because effectively this is what it is.

The meaning of life is fundamentally therefore, a mental concept of life. There can be no truth here. The mind uses the past and future to draw a pattern, showing the juxtapositioning and relationship between things. Therefore, the meaning of life is the pattern that the mind can draw around its experience of being.

Our minding of life gives us the ability to say it. Our saying of it is a uniquely human perspective which we cannot run away from, no matter how many new words we create; all the words and meaning ultimately come from us. Whatever we say about it, it will have the inevitability of anthropocentricity. The only meaning is how we can say it; this is the 'reality' that we create. Anything deeper than that still has the vanity of mankind attached to it. We cannot control it, only anticipate and tell the story.

The minding of something, is the comparing that comprises of the defining of something. If that something is 'life', then the comparing is either 'life with non-life' or 'lives with other lives'. This also is the meaning of life.

The Experience of Reality

The comparing of one's life with another is ego; most people spend their lives subscribed to this meaning. We could say that the meaning of life is to literally think about it.

The meaning of 'life' itself, is the story of how biology arose and will be superseded. We are to take a part in the latter.

The meaning of your personal life is up to you to find out. Think about it!

~

Feel your whole self, be aware of the sensation of all of you, and become aware of yourself as a fizzing form of energy manifested of the universe (not a part of the universe, but the whole of it condensed into this moment of sensory awareness—you are not separate to it or only a part of it, you are the whole of it). In this entheogenic state, you are God (though not with the skills that might be imagined for that role!). That is what our personal meaning of life is—to realise our being God.

*You cannot become enlightened until you recognise
that you already are.
You cannot enter paradise until you realise
that you are already there.*

It isn't out there; it is within you. It isn't in the future; it is in the absolute present. Do not be fooled by those who tell you you have to do something to know who you are. They can send you chasing your tail which can take up half your life before you realise that you already knew something but were being told that you didn't. There is nothing to gain or acquire. You are born complete. We knew and understood from the beginning but were told that we didn't by the adults who had forgotten themselves.

One Turning

If we don't start again from scratch in our philosophical searches, then all our concepts will be built upon an ad hoc assemblage of half-truths that we have acquired while growing up in an imperfect society. There's no point in looking for help from anyone else if you want to know the truth about yourself, they will only mislead you on your journey which only you can take in the discovery of who you really are. This is your meaning of life.

∼

Before I learnt to read I can remember being overawed at the concept of being able to read, believing that if I could do this mysterious magic, I would have access to the code of all those who have gone before me, and have the help which was meant for all those who have come after. All those previous enlightened versions of me passing on their age old and arcane help to me; messages personally for me—from angels. I used to stare at the strange looking shapes wondering what fantastic things they would reveal, how they would allow me to release the magic within me and become the magical being that I knew deep down that I was, because through these words I would have the means of accessing the divine and integrating into the manifestation.

The first of these divine beings that you are presented with in words as you are taught to read are Janet and John, or was it Jack and Jill; and after that it all just goes downhill, with me, pale, tumbling after.

But the messiah hasn't been yet. If he had, then my pre-reading assumptions would have been correct, and the societal system would have organised itself to give the right upbringing to those coming into the world. This has not been the case. How many thousands of years does it take? The society hasn't developed fully yet, and it's still growing. It has got to the point

The Experience of Reality

that it can be seen to be inevitable that it's going to be, to be the path towards heaven, the eutopia of the proper functioning of the Earth and human society.

We each are the manifestation of God, forbidden to be this in a society that dilutes us nearly eight billion times and doesn't teach us how to fully utilize our being. If we can't do it for ourselves, then we need to make sure that the following generations have the right conditions to maximise their potential and use their purposeful intention.

The meaning of our life collectively—as a society—is to create eutopia, where we assumed we already were when babies. Because anything less than heaven is a little bit of hell, just by the way of divisioning these parameters. Heaven is the parameter of future, coming from this present, and hell is anything less than it in our journey there. This now then, has a little bit of hell as we go through it, because it is less than heaven, because it is up to us to make it.

That's one way of saying it.

~

Creation becomes the creator.

Formation becomes the form.

Realizing becomes the reality.

Experience returns the same.

Turn One

netface.co.uk

Printed in Great Britain
by Amazon